Praise

'Accidental sexism is real. This is an important book and comes at just the right time. Well thought through, a good read and an accessible handbook.'
— **Air Marshal Andy Turner CB CBE**, Deputy Commander Capability, RAF

'In our "Collaborating with Men" research, men committed to gender equality often didn't know what they could do to contribute. We want them as allies in challenging current power structures. This book shows how men can be a part of the change we want.'
— **Dame Barbara Stocking**, President, Murray Edwards College, University of Cambridge

'As we tackle issues of sexism in the workplace, the majority of men who would never dream of acting inappropriately towards women need help to navigate the new world they find themselves in. This marvellous book is a self-help manual that explains the importance and the minefields of a diverse workforce in a way that is very easy to relate to. I recommend it to women as well. It explains a lot.'
— **Professor Dame Wendy Hall DBE** FRS FREng, Regius Professor of Computer Science, Executive Director, Web Science Institute, University of Southampton

'*The Accidental Sexist* is a portal to a necessary process of cultural change. Be in no doubt though, this has made me feel more than uncomfortable at times because certain behaviours, attitudes and beliefs are so ingrained (and aren't entirely wrong), but we simply must talk this through. I want to be an ally and not an accidental anything!'
— **Air Vice-Marshal (Retired) Michael Harwood CB CBE**

'This handbook is a great guide for leaders and managers who want to accelerate towards better performance, improved outcomes and happier teams. I found golden nuggets on every page.'
— **Mark Freed**, CEO, E2W

'Men: If you are confused, uncertain, hesitant or anxious about how to relate to new initiatives for greater gender equality in the workplace in these especially fraught times, this is the book for you! Simple practical advice on why being an ally to women and supporting gender equality will transform the workplace – and even improve your life!'
— **Michael Kimmel**, SUNY Distinguished Professor of Sociology and Gender Studies, Emeritus, Stony Brook University

'Much is written about diversity but a lot less about how men can play their part in equalising the playing field for women and minority voices. Having known of Gary's and Stephen's work over a number of years, I am delighted to see their learnings come together in a practical handbook which I would recommend to anyone looking to improve inclusion in their organisation.'

— **Jacqueline de Rojas CBE,**
President, techUK

'*The Accidental Sexist* demonstrates how heightening the awareness of and harnessing the power of the majority to alter the negative experiences of minorities is the most effective way to eradicate discrimination. I respect and admire any man who leans into this conversation with a curious mind and an open heart.'

— **Lynsey Campbell,** Technology Leader and Gender Equality Activist, Chairperson, Scotland Women in Technology

'There are a lot of organisations now that are committed to greater diversity, have put in place targets and unconscious bias training, but are still struggling to see real progress in terms of gender equality. This is especially true at the executive level. There are many men in those organisations that would like to see that change, and what *The Accidental Sexist* highlights so powerfully is how those men can be the solution and not the problem. It is the most practical guide I have ever read as to how to engage men in this programme in a way that is positive, inclusive and impactful for both men and women.'

— **Jeremy Cohen,** CEO, Dentons UK, Ireland and Middle East

The Accidental Sexist

A handbook for men on workplace diversity and inclusion

Gary Ford, Stephen Koch and Dr Jill Armstrong

R^ethink

First published in Great Britain in 2021
by Rethink Press (www.rethinkpress.com)

Contents

Introduction

This is a gender diversity and inclusion book about men. It outlines what happens when men talk to men about gender in the workplace – what men say and what men think. Now, given how the world works, do we really need another book all about men? The vast majority of history, literature, films and TV, and scientific research have centred around men – their experience, their bodies, their thoughts and beliefs – while the rest of the human population, slightly over 50%, have been largely ignored.

Why talk to men about gender?

So why are we writing, again, about men? Equality of opportunity in the workplace is a universal human subject, but men have largely been silent about it. Contrary to some people's belief, few men deliberately exclude or overlook women or try to impede their progress. In fact, if you suggest this to men, most are quite offended by the idea. The many ways in which women don't experience equality of opportunity are not obvious to men. Fundamentally, the idea that women working alongside them have experiences that are different to their own does not even occur to men most of the time. It is not deliberate, it is not even thoughtless; it is a void of thought. It does not exist.

Maybe this is not surprising because men have grown up in a world where, for generations, man's view is continuously written as 'the' view. Men don't set out to be sexist in their approach, but the outcomes of their behaviour *are* often sexist. It is completely accidental. That was what we – Gary and Stephen – came to realise when we started campaigning for gender equality of opportunity in the teams we led and worked alongside. This 'accidental sexism' inspired the title of this book.

Being an accidental sexist, however, does not remove accountability for its consequences. Yes, much has changed for the better over time but in countries such as the UK, US and India, when you look at the gender pay gap and who makes up the vast majority of leadership teams in relation to how many female managers are stuck in the middle of companies, too little has changed. When you consider the same issues for women of colour, the picture is even worse.

We certainly don't want to suggest that we have all the answers. But we will say that allowing most men to ignore the subject has not been a successful strategy. We have to get more men engaged in the conversation and try to increase their understanding of workplace gender inequality and why it is important. We want men to realise that working shoulder to shoulder with their colleagues, potential employees and female family members who do paid work, to bring about a more gender equal workplace is not only the right thing to do, it will make their lives better too.

This is a handbook on how to start that engagement with men. How to get them talking, keep them talking and help them act as allies for workplace gender equality. By 'acting as allies', we mean understanding the kinds of small, everyday incidents that add up to career death by a thousand paper cuts for those who have a less close fit with the dominant culture of their team or organisation.[1] We mean noticing when someone is not included, or when their behaviour is judged by a double standard, and acting to support them or tackle the barriers that stand in the way of equality of opportunity.

So, who is this handbook for? First, it is intended for men. Men who have experienced fewer barriers to belonging and men who have faced their own challenges. We want to encourage them to say, 'Yes, there are times when I've behaved like an accidental sexist' but to also say, 'I can change that.' We don't want men to feel blamed or guilty but to recognise that there may be gaps in their knowledge and there is more learning to do. We want them to feel that it's OK to be confused and uncertain and to not always know the right thing to do, because most of us feel like that. And when men recognise the barriers to gender inclusion, we want to provide good advice about what to do about this. What to do to widen the gender pool we are hiring from. To de-bias our promotion processes. To tackle the many ways in which the everyday behaviour of individuals means women often don't get the same opportunities to show their potential. To consider the influence of factors like who gets most airtime, who is in one's social circle and 'seems like a good guy', who is given the high-profile work. Over time, all of this shapes who managers decide to promote 'on merit'.

It would be great if women read this book too. Women who have thrived and women who have experienced that career death by a thousand paper cuts. We've had years of 'fixing' women to fit in with a man-made workplace, so we know many women are already attuned to gender equality issues. Both men and women have been influenced by deep-rooted social expectations of gender roles so both men and women can behave in accidentally sexist ways. Please encourage the men and women in your life to read it, as it provides some useful, practical tips on things that we can all do differently to be more inclusive and create more equitable workplaces.

Lastly, the book is also designed to be read by business and community leaders who want to make inclusion a priority but either don't know the best way of doing that or have found that what they have tried so far, isn't working well enough. Even if what you are doing is working, some of our suggestions may still help.

We can all – men and women – behave like accidental sexists, whether we are willing to admit it or not. The most important question is: what are you going to do about it?

Our manifesto for change

The business case for change is clear. Multiple studies show that companies that genuinely embrace diversity and inclusion are more profitable, have greater innovation and deliver a better customer experience.[2,3,4] They are less likely to damage their reputation by causing health and safety issues, have a more engaged and motivated workforce and are more likely to gain new clients.

Given all those benefits, why aren't things changing faster? Why are so many companies not making significant inroads into their gender pay gap? Why, in 2020, did we only have seven female CEOs of FTSE 250 companies (down from nine in 2017) and none of them women of colour?[5] In America, only one in twenty-five C-suite executives are women of colour.[6] Why do women make up only 8.3% of executive directorships in FTSE 250 companies?[7] Why, when women are well represented in the middle-management level of many sectors, do they become increasingly scarce the further up the corporate tree you look? For example, in 317 American companies investigated by McKinsey and Company in 2020, women made up 38% of managers but only 21% of the C-suite.[8]

Are companies allocating the right level of investment to the areas that will make a difference? Many organisations have focused on diversity, which typically translates to hiring more women and people of colour. It's time to focus just as hard on inclusion. By inclusion we mean the sense of belonging and being valued, which everyone should expect but takes work to achieve. We mean inclusion for anyone who feels excluded by the majority culture because of their gender, ethnicity, religion, sexuality or disability. Without that sense of belonging and of being assessed fairly based on their contribution, many of your diverse hires will become demoralised, disengaged and will disappear.

We've noticed that a lot of companies talk about having a diversity and inclusion (D&I) strategy. They publish great material on their corporate websites explaining that strategy and the importance of their values. But is this enough? It is easy to have a few sponsored events or run short online training courses on unconscious bias, but real inclusion must be deeply embedded in the culture and the way that everyone does business.

Anyone in a management or leadership position needs to invest time in learning about and understanding inclusion. We all know that gender inequalities in society exist, but how many people have taken the time to understand how this manifests in their workplace? To read the research and allocate resources to discussion and dialogue? To fully comprehend how cognitive biases affect how they work, the decisions that they make and how engaged or motivated they feel? Without deep learning, we are never going to change hearts, minds and behaviour.

Critically, delivering inclusion requires more than raising awareness and understanding. This is only the start. Yes, the organisation's processes and systems need to change. It's also vital that people know what you want them to do differently every day. Changing behaviour tends to lead to changes in attitude, not the other way around.

In short, inclusion and equality of opportunity is not just a problem for women, it is a problem for everyone. Men who are part of the mainstream can no longer remain bystanders when others are not treated equitably. Why? Because there is much to gain for men who act as allies.

What's in it for men?

Becoming an ally for inclusion carries a number of benefits for men.[9,10] Here are a few:

1. **It will improve your emotional intelligence:** Trying to understand how someone might think differently to you and then how you can improve their experience will help develop you as a coach and a leader.

2. **You will work in teams which are more productive, creative and perform better collectively:**[11] This is the benefit of diversity of thought that comes with teams who have different viewpoints and experiences and whose contribution is encouraged and respected.

3. **You will build better teams who will build better products and services:** Improving the balance of your team by increasing diversity will increase both your own and your team's learning potential. The more diverse thinking that goes into the development of a product or service you provide, the more attractive it will be to a wider audience, bringing in more customers, more revenue and more rewards.

4. **You will be better at your job:** Embracing a different worldview can help you become a more effective manager. Even if you're not in a management position and don't consider yourself to be a leader, this can still help you in your career by enabling you to deal with people in a far more effective way.

5. **It will enhance your personal relationships:** As you get better at having more open and equal conversations with other employees, you will build better relationships with them. It will also enhance the relationships you have with those around you outside of work – your partner, your children and your friends.

6. **It can increase your personal resilience:** Being an ally will enable you to build a support network with people both inside and outside of work who will be supportive when times are tough.

7. **It can smash the 'man box':**[12] Challenging gender expectations helps men to be more involved with their family lives, to live a fuller life outside of work and helps relieve the mental and physical toll of being expected to be the bread-winner, to be ambitious and put work first.

8. **You get to have more fun in the workplace:** We've been to many great events with a diversity and inclusion theme, it makes everyone feel good and you come away energised and motivated.

All organisations seek to improve the performance of their people and this is only possible when people feel welcomed, respected and valued, irrespective of and because of their diverse contributions. Diversity of thought comes from diversity in people's gender identity, race, ethnicity, upbringing, social class, personality type and so on. Diversity of thought encourages richer debate, fuller explanations of ideas and thinking, more rigorous challenge and better execution of better decisions. Diversity and inclusion drive successful teams and productive organisations which is good for men, good for us all.

Why us?

Ten years ago, if you had said to either of us (Stephen and Gary) that we would become male allies for gender equality, we probably would have laughed. Sure, working within technology, it was clear there were fewer women than men. But was that our problem? As fathers of daughters, we would have recognised the need to ensure equality of opportunity for all children. But was there a wider problem that we needed to address? Surely the equal opportunities agenda had done its job? Since then, though, various things changed to move us from complacency to active participation.

Gary

'My journey to becoming a male ally for gender equality started around five years ago. The firm I worked for began to recognise that not only was there a lack of women in technology, but the problem was getting worse. The company had around 50,000 people working in technology at the time, with just over 20% being women. We decided to set up a new networking group: Women In Technology (WIT). As a senior leader in the firm, I was asked to be one of the sponsors of WIT.

'I have to admit that, for the first few months, I was quite a passive sponsor. I would get together with the team once a month or so to review strategy, objectives and progress, as well as joining a monthly networking event. I was often the only man joining fifty women in a room (an ironic mirroring of many women's experience in IT).

'During those early months we looked at research, heard from academics and business leaders, watched TED Talks and read books. We were educating ourselves on the reasons why fewer women than men study computer science at school and university and why, if they did take a role in IT, they often did not stay and quit far more frequently than men.[13,14] As I became more and more fascinated by the subject, I began to realise just how deeply uneducated I was.

'Until then, I'd thought of myself as a decent manager, someone who treated everyone in his team fairly and equally. Our research on gender equality made me realise that I hadn't thought properly about the lived experience of large numbers of my team – and not just the women.

'Two things were becoming abundantly clear to me. First, I was now on a powerful learning journey about diversity and inclusion. Second, there were few men in this conversation, and they were the ones most in need of it.

'I can honestly say that my work as a male ally has made me a better manager, a better coach, a better leader, a better father, a better partner and a better friend. A better human being.'

Stephen

'My journey started at a similar time to Gary's where the company I worked at had an alpha male culture which increasingly made me uncomfortable. There were fewer women in leadership roles than I would have expected. I tried to support the WIT group but saw that only a subset of women attended the events, and few men. As I spoke to more and more women in the organisation,

I realised there were problems and biases creeping into meetings and management decisions that were impacting women, and this became increasingly visible to me. While we were focused on getting women into the organisation, often their experiences once they joined weren't particularly positive, and we needed to do something about it.

'I also realised that if we wanted to improve inclusion at the firm, we wouldn't be able to do it by engaging only a subset of the women in the organisation. We needed the majority of people to be involved, which meant we needed to find a way to engage the men in understanding the problem and thinking about what could be changed. Talking to the men in the organisation, it became clear that a lot of the problematic behaviours went unnoticed.

'Having a strong sense of fair play and wanting the firm to be somewhere where everyone would feel comfortable and able to succeed, I resolved to try and find some like-minded individuals to see what could be done.'

In 2016, in partnership with our female colleagues, we decided to form a Male Allies group for WIT. The focus of the initiative was to encourage more men to engage in discussions about gender equality and to partner with female colleagues to understand why so few women choose to work within technology. Capturing feedback from women on their experiences, our small team created a powerful and engaging workshop that allowed men to explore their attitudes towards women as well as wider diversity and inclusion topics.

By the end of 2017, this workshop had been delivered to over 1,000 men within the company, and the programme was extended into Singapore, India, Argentina and the US in 2018. In September 2018, following its success in technology, a Male Allies programme across the whole firm was launched.

Our programme has changed the way we think and, hopefully, how we behave in both life and business. Our mission is to share our experience with others in the hope that they will be inspired to go on a similar journey.

Perspective

We do not intend to give the impression that we are representing half of the planet, that our messages are what *all* men are thinking and saying. We are sharing our experiences, and those of our small cohort of enlightened partners, of talking to thousands of men and hundreds of women about their lived experiences. We have summarised our findings under a few key themes, but this is by no means a definitive view of the male experience. We have learned much, but there is a tremendous amount more still to learn.

We also do not want to give the impression to women that we are 'mansplaining' their oppression to them. That is not our objective. We work in partnership with women, not for them. Suggesting that women want or need men to 'help' them would only add to the problem. Many women are thriving in their careers. Our aim is to work to undo a decades-old power imbalance and overcome the unconscious bias it has caused. To this end, we are sharing the challenges faced by some of the women we've talked to so that men can understand more about the lived experience of their female colleagues. In this spirit of partnership, the third author of this book is Dr Jill Armstrong.

Jill

'My contribution to this book draws from the five years I've spent leading the "Collaborating with Men" research project at Murray Edwards College, University of Cambridge. Early on, to our surprise, we found that the female alumnae of our college felt that inhospitable workplace culture had a more negative effect on their career progress than balancing work and family life. We dug into this and found that many women felt that they did not fit in, were overlooked or had to try harder and be better than their male colleagues to get promoted, or were held to a different standard.

'When we looked, we found that little research had been done on men's views of the kinds of challenges being reported by women. That prompted us to survey men about their perceptions of the everyday outcomes of unconscious gender bias and compare men's views with women's. The gender differences in perceptions that emerged were a great place to start conversations in workshops that we ran in many workplaces, across sectors, about how to tackle these issues not only at a company level but also seeking to change the way individuals behave.

'After launching our reports, I was invited to speak at many events on diversity and inclusion. This is how I met Stephen and Gary and learned about their impressive Male Allies programme. I believe that the problem of workplace gender equality will only be solved by men and women working together. That's why I'm delighted to add my voice to this book. It draws on my knowledge of academic research on gender inequalities in the workplace. My contribution particularly focuses on everyday accidental sexisms and biases and what men say about diversity and inclusion at work. I have also offered many suggestions about how individuals and teams can change their behaviour to build more inclusive cultures.'

What we mean by 'gender'

Throughout this book, when we write about men and women we are referring to how others see and label the gender of their work colleagues. The terms 'men' and 'women' do not encompass the entirety of the spectrum that is gender. We know that transgender men and women experience challenges that are not covered here. We also recognise that there are people who do not identify with either the male or female genders. We apologise if we have offended anyone and, if this has happened, we would appreciate hearing from you to add to our learning.

This rather gender binary approach is due to our focus on engaging male allies. It also reflects something we want to challenge about inclusion in the workplace: that people are siloed into 'interest groups' – in this case, 'women'. Inclusion should reflect the way women's identities overlap (our gender, ethnicity, race, social class, religion and so on). This is often called 'intersectionality'. We particularly need to consider the experience of women of colour because they face greater challenges attributable to their membership of other under-represented groups. There is overlap with the experiences of white women but the issues faced are not the same. This book is focused on gender inclusion because that is our area of expertise. That said, we make many suggestions about actions that we can take together, for the benefit of all. Of course, different solutions for different groups of people are also needed. We believe wholeheartedly in the importance of inclusion across all groups, whether you identify them by gender, race, social class, religion, a medical condition or any other characteristic that can put people in the 'out' group or get in the way of equitable access to opportunities in the workplace.

Much of this book is about how you get men (particularly the majority group of straight, white men) into the conversation. We find gender a pretty good starting point for the conversation. And often it will lead to those men more readily embracing other diverse groups that are different to them that they might once have avoided or ignored. So although it's a start, we recognise that it is not where we need to end. As you will see, we had to embrace difficult conversations at the start of our journey as you will yours, but the more you do it, the easier it becomes. This is one of the biggest lessons we learned – have more conversations and get more used to being uncomfortable.

What can you expect from this book?

We, Stephen, Gary and Jill, aim to give people – though especially men, and particularly those in positions of authority or influence – some practical suggestions of things they can do differently that will help their working lives (and hopefully their personal lives too).

This book will:

1. Help people, particularly men, understand why gender equality and broader inclusion in the workplace are so important

2. Share feedback from female colleagues on their lived experience, making it clear that things need to change

3. Offer our learning and resources to help others become better educated on equality, diversity and inclusion (see our Useful Resources at the end of the book)

4. Share our insights into what men are thinking and saying about gender equality

5. Give advice to anyone who wants to create a male allies programme for gender equality or equality for under-represented groups

6. Most importantly, offer practical ideas for what companies and individuals can do to build a more inclusive environment

In the following chapters, we will share our experience of what happens when you try to get men engaged in this conversation, what they say, what they think (or at least what they say they think) and how they react. We find out what happens when we tell them that it's not only the right thing to do but also how it will help them and what they can do differently.

We will outline what individuals, leaders within organisations, and organisations themselves can do to start solving some of the problems we've identified. We will talk about how to get men engaged and what conversations need to happen; about how men and women need to work in partnership to create better workplace outcomes for everyone.

We will provide practical tips that individuals and teams can follow that will help with everyday inclusion, and explain how to change hiring practices to reduce the impact of bias and attract a more diverse workforce. We will advise on how people managers, who play a pivotal role in implementing and reinforcing culture change, can help everyone in their team feel included. Finally, we will provide ideas on how organisations can make these cultural changes stick so that inclusion comes naturally.

Thank you all for picking up this particular book to read, we hope you enjoy it. If you find it to be of value to you, you have further ideas, or even if you strongly disagree with something we've said, we would love to hear from you. Our education on this subject has only just begun.

A key message for anyone reading this book is: please treat this as part of your learning journey. No matter how senior, how experienced, how well-intentioned you may be, there is always more to learn. We hope you will agree.

Chapter 1

What's The Problem?

Contrary to what many believe, gender equality isn't a done deal in the workplace. Neither in women's representation overall, nor in women's representation in senior leadership roles. When women are recruited, they face greater challenges in getting the promotions they seek and feeling that they belong. This chapter looks at the evidence supporting these claims.

Where are the women?

Many industries continue to be dominated by men. And yes, we know there are industries and sectors which tend to have more women than men – we used to joke in our company about setting up a female allies group for men in HR – yet even in HR the numbers drop when you look at the executive level. Research by Emily Burt from the People Management company highlighted this issue: 'We ran a survey that showed about a 70% imbalance in favour of females in the lower to mid ranks, and then about 70% males in the mid to senior ranks.'[1]

Much work has been done to encourage more women into career paths traditionally dominated by men. The number of women achieving STEM (science, technology, engineering and maths) qualifications has increased, but looking at the UK 2018/19 university graduation figures, women made up only 29% of the students with core STEM qualifications and took only 24% of the total number of STEM-based working roles.[2] The US also has a lack of women in a number of STEM degrees, including computer science and engineering (see illustration below). The country that produces the highest percentage of female STEM graduates is India, at over 40%. Unfortunately, only 30% of these enter the workforce and a mere 14% of the scientists in research institutions in India are women.[3]

Despite more women entering the workforce, more women achieving higher education qualifications in STEM subjects and more women working in

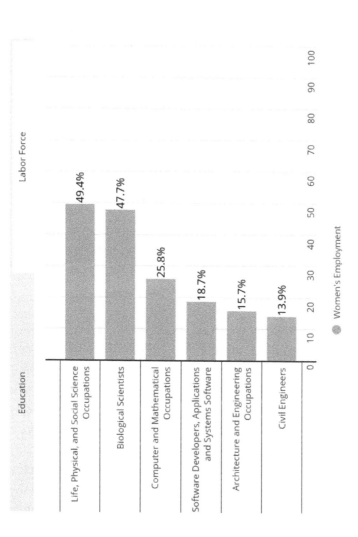

Education   Labor Force

- Life, Physical, and Social Science Occupations: **49.4%**
- Biological Scientists: **47.7%**
- Computer and Mathematical Occupations: **25.8%**
- Software Developers, Applications and Systems Software: **18.7%**
- Architecture and Engineering Occupations: **15.7%**
- Civil Engineers: **13.9%**

0   10   20   30   40   50   60   70   80   90   100

● Women's Employment

The gender gap in STEM[4]

STEM-based roles, women continue to be significantly under-represented in key industries such as technology, engineering, construction, manufacturing and transportation.[5] Looking beyond STEM to all sectors, across all companies there are also far fewer women than men in leadership roles. Female chief executive officers (CEOs) are still relatively rare. As of May 2020 only 7.4% of the CEOs of the Fortune 500 companies were women.[6] With government pressure, the UK FTSE 250 is making progress on improving diversity in boardrooms, with the executive committees and their direct reports increasing from 25.2% women in 2017 to 28.6% in 2019. Key roles, however, remain male-dominated, with just 12% of chief information officers (CIOs) being women and just 16% of chief financial officers (CFOs).[7]

Despite efforts in many sectors to recruit more women, gender imbalances persist in more senior roles. Our working experience is in financial services. Over the last fifteen years, banks have increased initiatives and programmes to recruit more female graduates and, for a number of them, women now make up over 40% of graduates in entry-level positions, including in areas of historically poor diversity, such as information technology.[8] Nevertheless, financial services companies still struggle to retain, promote and develop women. A report commissioned by the

UK government referred to 'a permafrost' preventing women rising from the middle tier of management in the financial services sector where, in 2015, women made up only 14% of Executive Committees. We continue to see the workforce gender diversity in banks reducing as roles become more senior.[9] This is an issue in many sectors. Even when women are well represented in managerial or professional roles, they are proportionally poorly represented at the most senior levels. In the UK, women account for 50% of lawyers but only 28% are partners in private practice.[10]

When it comes to promotion into managerial roles, men are more likely than women to make it onto the first rung of the ladder. McKinsey and Company's research carried out among 600 American businesses shows that for every 100 men hired or promoted into managerial roles there are only 72 women.[11]

The chart below from the same report illustrates the issue clearly.

This trend continues over time. KPMG's research among FTSE 100 and 250 companies, which tracked career progress over time, showed that men were 4.5 times more likely to make it onto the executive committee compared with women who started their

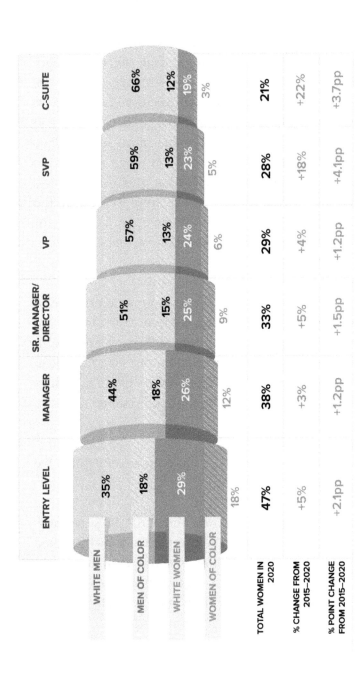

The gender gap in promotions[12]

careers at the same time.[13] In our experience, most managers, male and female, think that they promote on merit, so what is going wrong?

When talking to people about why this disparity occurs, many people assume that fewer women make it to the senior levels of an organisation because of career breaks taken to have children and the responsibilities of childcare, which typically falls on women. While this is a factor, there are many other reasons. More focus is needed internally within companies on the retention and promotion of women and on reviewing policies, processes and the behaviour of male and female managers to look for bias and to work to correct it.

We have an example that clearly illustrates some of the biases that are in play. A woman who we met at a conference told us about how, as the co-chair of the women's group at her firm, she met with one of the most senior men in her UK organisation (part of a global firm). After a good meeting where she took him through the initiatives she was planning for the group, his parting comment to her was: 'This is great and I hope we'll see more senior women in our leadership ranks soon. We may still need a few of us alpha males to make sure we still are able to make the big decisions quickly.'

How accidental gender bias works

Careers are personal and when things aren't going well, we all have a tendency to think, 'It's just me' or, 'I don't get on with my boss.' However, many challenges are more common to certain groups of people than we realise.

There is a clear link between the lack of proportional representation of women in the most senior roles and unconscious bias. That is, the attitudes towards and expectations of men and women that derive from social norms formed long ago and built up over decades, which continue to influence our behaviour now. Take the example of women's football. After the First World War, many women's football teams and leagues sprang up. Women played in international matches and were well supported and often watched by bigger crowds than the men's game. One of the best teams, Dick, Kerr Ladies FC, played a match at Goodison Park (the ground of Everton, a male team) in 1920 that attracted a crowd of 53,000 with thousands more outside, unable to get in. The UK Football Association objected to the growing popularity of the women's game and, in 1921, banned all football grounds from hosting their matches. The statement they issued said football was 'Quite unsuitable for females and ought not to be encouraged.' The women's teams melted away at every level and this long absence has made it extremely difficult for the modern women's game to attract fans and funding to play the world's most popular sport.[14]

Most of us aren't aware of how these biases act on us, which is why we are using the term 'accidental bias'. So what are the common accidental gender biases that are evident in the workplace and how do they influence people's everyday experiences? It's important to say that research shows women judge other women by gender-skewed criteria too.[15] However, men are much more likely to be in senior positions, so have an important role to play in tackling these challenges.

The main accidental gender biases uncovered by academic scholarship are remarkably consistent across cultures. For clarity, these biases can be summarised as the 5Cs:

1. Capability

2. Constraint

3. Communication

4. Connections

5. Credit

The table below presents the biases and their implications.[16,17]

The 5Cs

1) Capability	2) Constraint	
Role Congruence Bias Female strengths thought to be conscientiousness, attention to detail, good relationship management	Ability Bias Male strengths thought to be leadership, commitment to work and technical, maths and science skills	Benevolent Sexism Well-intentioned men often treat women more carefully or make decisions on their behalf, taking away control
Leads to women being:		
• *Less likely* to be given high-profile responsibilities • *More likely* to be given admin tasks or tasks less critical to P&L • *More likely* to be negatively judged for behaving in ways that are more expected of men (eg speaking up, being assertive, showing ambition)	• *Less likely* to be judged to merit promotion into leadership positions • *More likely* to be promoted on past experience, rather than judgements about future potential	• *Less likely* to be considered for opportunities when they have young children • *Less likely* to be given direct or actionable feedback • *More likely* to be questioned and expected to provide more evidence of their competence

3) Communication	4) Connections	5) Credit
Language Bias Women find it harder to be heard and corporate language often carries the message 'be more like a man'	Affinity Bias Our tendency to associate and bond with those with whom we have more in common	Performance Bias When women are in the minority they are judged not as individuals, but as representatives of their gender

Leads to women being:

• *Less likely* to get airtime in meetings • *More likely* to be interrupted • *More likely* to not be heard and to have their contributions credited to someone else • *More likely* to be the target of 'banter' • *More likely* to be called sexist names when they speak out	• *Less likely* to be given opportunities or sponsored for career progression • *More likely* to be side-lined in workplace social networks • *Less likely* to have a strong profile with the most senior people in the organisation	• *More likely* to be punished more harshly for mistakes/ under-performance • *More likely* to be thought to owe their position to diversity quotas rather than merit

Our conversations with members of a 'Women in Technology' (WIT) network produced examples of these biases. We saw **ability** and **role congruence bias** in the comments and assumptions reported by women in technical roles, such as:

- When entering a technical project meeting, being greeted with 'Are you the business analyst?' – this assumes that the woman is not technical.

- 'If we need to improve documentation we should have some females in the team.'

- 'You're a coder, really?'

- 'This will be a technical meeting so you might like to bring a technical member of your team.'

- A woman who worked as a technical architect explained how, whenever she presented a new technical design to her team, a male colleague felt the need to continuously interrupt and 'explain' what she was saying.

Role congruence bias was also evident in the assumption that women will take on more of the work equivalent to housework in the workplace. Women reported that they were expected to do a much higher percentage of the administrative work compared to men in the same roles. Examples of this include organising social events, taking follow-up actions at meetings, doing more of the documentation and less of the programming. Placing more of this administrative burden on women is taxing their time and slowing down their career progression because they have less time to do the work that would put them in the frame for promotion.

We also found that, assuming women had more work to do at home, managers also assumed that women had less motivation and were less able to commit to their careers. This bias is known as **benevolent sexism**. It can be well-meaning, but takes control away from the women concerned. As a result, women reported that they were less likely to be chosen for new projects and roles that required longer hours or business travel, and managers kept a closer eye on the time they spent in the office/face-time than on the quality and quantity of work they produced. Examples shared with us included when a late-running project requires the whole team to work the weekend, the female member of the team is not asked, and assuming women won't or shouldn't work after having a baby, with comments like 'Thank you for all your hard work, we wish you the best of luck for the future,' or 'Why are you still working?' We have even heard examples of where women were asked by their managers if they could think of anyone suitable for a stretch assignment where they had to reply, 'What about me?'

We saw **performance bias** in judgements made about women as a group, rather than as individuals, and in put-downs about being a 'diversity hire', such as:

- 'You're in the right demographic to be going for promotion.'
- 'We need more women to brighten the team up.'
- When returning from attending a diversity initiative, 'Back from your women's thing, then. What do you do there? Stick pins into dolls of men?'
- 'It is much easier for females to get hired on the graduate programme.'

We saw **affinity** bias in comments about feeling excluded from the 'in group'. Some examples were women being ignored when they arrived in the office, rather than greeted and asked about their weekend. Some teams would discuss football and would roll their eyes if anyone brought up kids. Other teams would have certain lunch or social patterns that the majority enjoyed but the minority were excluded from, either by accidentally not being invited or because social events were mostly focused around drinking or playing single-gender sports or were held at times that meant women were less likely to attend, because women tend to have bigger networks of friends to see outside work and are more likely to work part-time. Other everyday experiences included:

- Feeling ignored, silenced and left out of conversations

- Receiving a less enthusiastic greeting from the team than male colleagues

- 'I feel like when I go over to speak to him, I'm just having a conversation with the back of his head'

These behaviours cause problems. First, it can make the workplace feel unwelcoming – if you don't fit the mould of the managers or team leaders; you feel like you shouldn't be there. Second, it can easily spill over into the decision-making process for male managers, with the result that, if they are asked to think of a person for a challenging project they will tend to think of male candidates first.

Most men aren't deliberately acting in a way that puts obstacles in women's way. In fact, when men hear comments like this from their female colleagues many are shocked. The issue is, if you don't experience these challenges then you tend not to know that they exist. As research, conducted by Jill for Murray Edwards College, University of Cambridge, shows a far larger proportion of women than men notice the impact of these accidental biases.[18] This is because women's careers are more likely to be negatively impacted by the gender stereotypes that lurk in our collective minds.

Three examples of the findings of the Murray Edwards College research are given below.

Affinity bias

Women believe that their male colleagues have better access to career sponsorship from senior leaders. The gender gap in this belief is widest when comparing the responses of senior women and senior men:[19]

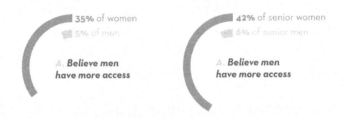

Q. Do you believe that males in your workplace have had more access than females to sponsorship from senior leaders?

35% of women
5% of men

A. *Believe men have more access*

42% of senior women
6% of senior men

A. *Believe men have more access*

Murray Edwards College 'Collaborating with Men' research. [n.5737 (all sectors). 53% men, 47% women.]

Performance bias

Women believe that they are judged more negatively when they behave in the same way as men. Men notice this less than women:[20]

Q. The same behaviour can be judged more negatively if you are a woman. How often have you noticed this happening?

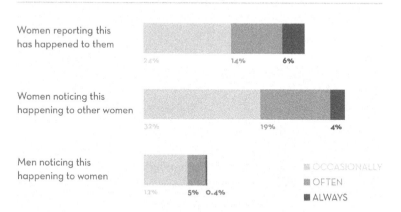

Women reporting this has happened to them

24% 14% 6%

Women noticing this happening to other women

32% 19% 4%

Men noticing this happening to women

12% 5% 0.4%

■ OCCASIONALLY
■ OFTEN
■ ALWAYS

Murray Edwards College 'Collaborating with Men' research. [Respondents agreeing always, often or occasionally. n.6466 that this has happened in their workplace in the past 12 months.]

Role congruence bias

More than half of the women surveyed believed that women's career progress suffers as a result of stereotypical views about female strengths and traits. By contrast, more than half of the men surveyed believed this rarely or never happens.[21]

Q. Do you think that traits that women are thought more likely to possess, such as building good relationships, attention to detail and strong skills in administration lead to them being perceived in your workplace as good managers rather than good potential leaders?

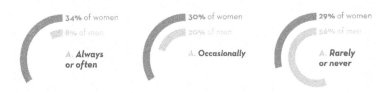

34% of women
8% of men
A. Always or often

30% of women
20% of men
A. Occasionally

29% of women
56% of men
A. Rarely or never

Murray Edwards College 'Collaborating with Men' research. [n.6651 49% men, 51% women. NB. Don't knows not presented.]

Some of these attitudes and behaviours (often called micro-inequities or micro-aggressions) that impact workplace culture may seem trivial, but other academic research tells us that they can have equally negative outcomes for the careers of individuals as overt (and illegal) forms of discrimination.[22] Repeated experience of behaviour that is perceived as unfair chips away at morale, confidence and good humour, becomes exhausting to deal with, contributes to feelings of not belonging and can result in women deciding to move on or getting stuck in mid-level roles.

What holds men back from engaging?

Four big things get in the way of supportive men taking active steps to build more gender-inclusive workplaces. First, as we've just discussed, a widespread lack of understanding that their workplaces aren't the meritocracy they believe them to be.

Second, the view that motherhood (or the potential for motherhood) gets in the way of ambition and that women choose home over work. Women do make more career compromises than men because they often act as the primary parent. Many studies have shown that women do a much higher share of the unpaid work at home compared to men, whether that's household chores or caring for children and/or elderly relatives. A survey of 20,000 women in the UK in July 2020 also found that 72% of working mothers had to work fewer hours due to lack of childcare in the Covid-19 pandemic.[23]

However, the assumption that motherhood is a career limitation is an over-simplification. Many mothers are ambitious and successfully balance work and parenthood, just as men do. Far from all women are mothers. By the age of 45, 19% of UK women remain child-free, and this figure is rapidly increasing.[24] Numbers of single-sex parenting partners are increasing. More men now want and expect to be hands-on parents and share domestic responsibilities with their female partners. This over-simplification results in labelling female employees as 'high risk' in conversations about promotions, and comments about 'maternity risk', women being 'at that age' or having a 'childcare risk'.

Both the false belief in a meritocracy and the assumptions around motherhood result in many men thinking that the remaining barriers to gender equality at work are 'women's issues' largely related to working motherhood and are therefore not relevant to them and not something they want or need to be involved with.

The third main barrier is that a surprisingly large cohort of men, particularly white men, think that there is now positive discrimination, meaning that women and other under-represented groups are being handed an unfair advantage over their white male colleagues. It is worth highlighting an Ernst and Young survey (2017) of over 1,000 full-time employees in the US, which showed that 35% of respondents thought that the focus on diversity meant that white men were being overlooked for promotion.[25]

Yet, if you look into the data on hiring and promotions for most companies, there is usually little evidence to support fears that men are being discriminated against. One reason why men might believe they are being disadvantaged relates to the promotion process. Many firms try to correct for conscious and unconscious bias in their promotion process, for example by looking at the diversity of potential candidates managers are recommending for promotion. If there is little diversity of candidates and especially if the candidate pool under-represents the diversity of the level they are being promoted from, managers are asked to review their promotion lists with diversity in mind.

This instruction to managers to look again at the diversity of candidates for promotion can be miscommunicated, particularly if it has to travel through multiple layers of the organisation. The message can end up being understood as, 'I have to find more women to add to the promotion list.' The instruction to check that candidates represent the demographic of the group should be given carefully to convey the manager's responsibility to check that they have been as unbiased as possible in the selection process. Even if the manager interprets this instruction correctly, they don't always take the time to communicate this to their teams. We have seen many cases where the manager asks someone in their team if they know of any women or other diverse candidates for promotion; that person may draw the – incorrect – conclusion that the manager is working to a quota.

This type of perspective, where actions in your favour are ignored and actions that look like they favour others are given undue importance, can be partly explained by the headwind bias.[26,27] Psychologically, we all tend to be much more aware of barriers and hindrances that need to be overcome than of benefits that can be enjoyed. This tendency to overstate the impact of hindrances also leads Democrats and Republicans to both claim the electoral map is biased against them, and most sports fans to believe their teams are adversely affected by the match schedule while their rivals are benefiting.

Finally, the fourth issue is that when men are supportive of workplace gender equality, they often don't know what they can do to help achieve it. Hence the need for this book.

The price men pay

Men do not often consider how gender stereotyping negatively affects them, so can be surprised about how significant the consequences can be. There is a growing body of research that shows how the challenge of living up to masculine norms can put severe strain on men's mental health. Research from Catalyst showed how the need to 'be a winner', 'never show weakness', 'be a man's man' and 'avoid all things feminine', can lead to men:[28]

- Focusing on career advancement by sacrificing relationships with friends and family, which can mean a loss of important psychological support

- Not seeking support when faced with anxiety, depression or illness

- Taking unnecessary safety risks to demonstrate their toughness

- Being rejected or paying a high social cost for not conforming

It is, therefore, unsurprising that men often pay a price in terms of both physical health (eg a reluctance to proactively attend medical checks) and mental health, when they are confronted daily with representations in the media of the 'ideal man', that none of us can ever live up to. That suicide is the biggest killer of men under the age of fifty in the UK is a staggering statistic that men should stop and take note of.[29] The same is true in many other countries. In the US, the suicide rate is highest in middle-aged white men; white males account for around 70% of all suicides in the US, and men are 3.5 times more likely than women to die by suicide.[30] In India, male suicides are roughly twice as high as female suicides.[31]

Unfortunately, Stephen has direct experience of this in the workplace: 'Over the last ten years working in investment banking I've typically managed teams of up to around 120–150 people but, despite these teams being relatively small, two male team members have committed suicide in the last ten years.'

More active conversations about gender equality can go a long way to helping men confront these norms and encourage them to bring issues of health and well-being into much greater focus. It is important to do this in the context of engaging your whole workforce on how to build a more inclusive environment, and make it clear that this is a discussion that involves everyone and aims to make a difference for everyone, not just women and traditionally under-represented groups.

Key takeaways

These are the key challenges that need addressing:

- A number of male-dominated industries have developed a culture that is unwelcoming to women.

- Even in sectors where the workforce is more gender balanced, women are still far less likely to hold senior positions.

- Despite many government- and organisation-led initiatives, progress in attracting more women to certain sectors or hiring or promoting women to senior positions in all sectors, is happening at a glacial pace.

- Gender biases are inherited from wider society. Individual men and women often act in accidentally sexist ways which mean women face more challenges to their career progress than men. Genuinely meritocratic organisations are rare.

- Men are far more likely to be in leadership positions that allow them to effect cultural change, but they are frequently not engaged with diversity and inclusion initiatives.

- A lot of men actively resist diversity and inclusion in the workplace because they believe it is detrimental to their careers.

- More and more men state that they want a better balance between their work and personal lives and to play a more active role in bringing up their children, but stereotypical male cultural norms frequently prevent them from doing so.

We have to find ways to make people understand that inequality of opportunity is still much more likely to be experienced by women than men. That non-inclusive behaviours are still happening, and are happening around you, every day.

The next chapter deals with getting the men in your organisation engaged in this conversation.

Chapter 2

Engaging Men As Allies

Talking to men about diversity can be a challenge, particularly if you find, as we did, that most of them don't participate in your organisation's current diversity events. In this chapter, we describe how we went about engaging with men; how we found them, what we found worked and what didn't, what we talked about and what we learned from those initial discussions.

Getting started

Like many organisations, across our firm men were typically not engaging with diversity and inclusion groups. Our discussions with senior women made us realise that, unless we started engaging the people who were making the daily decisions on hiring, career development, promotions and compensation, then changing the culture and making our workplace more inclusive would remain elusive. Our aim became to engage this silent, mainly male, population in our company.

Our first step was to find a handful of passionate people to get things started. They proved to be a mixture of (mostly) men and women. It is important that men step forward and provide proactive leadership and drive if you are to successfully engage them in large numbers. We recruited men who were already sponsoring women in the organisation, men who had daughters, men who were role models for flexible working or who had taken shared parental leave. We looked for men who already had a female mentor or had demonstrated a commitment to building diverse teams, for example by hiring plenty of women. Those with experience of managing teams had the most to contribute; we needed their management experience to understand the issues, but we also had to make sure they could give their time to help. The group also needed a clearly defined purpose and set of actions to take, and its members needed to be senior enough to help overcome some of the barriers to getting initiatives like this started.

Once we had created the group, the next step was to decide what to call ourselves.

What's in a name?

We originally called the group the Male Advocate Network, or MAN. This name seemed to polarise opinion – some men and a few women liked it, but most didn't. We had discussions about the word 'advocate' versus the word 'ally'; advocate feels a lot more active, but plays into the stereotype of women needing help. The way we define an ally is 'someone in a position of relative power and influence who acts in solidarity with and alongside a more marginalised group or individual.' This seemed to describe the support we were looking to provide, and it also provoked fewer negative reactions.

In the end, we called the group Male Allies, for a few reasons. It sends a positive signal, suggesting equal partners, a clear move away from 'fixing the women'. The choice was also influenced by the fact that in our company there had been a lot of success with a Pride Allies programme to support the LGBTQ+ community, so we already had a model we could leverage. The next step was to get out and find more allies.

Recruiting male allies

Our steering group used a couple of tactics to recruit allies. The first was to reach out to existing groups involved with diversity and inclusion to find men already involved in existing initiatives who would be interested to help. The next thing we tried was to use a regular women's network event and make it a 'bring a man' session. This worked well in Gary's office:

> 'All of the fifty or sixty women who came to the monthly WIT session were asked to bring a male colleague. Some of them had to forcibly march those men to the conference room, but once there, we had a really engaging session. For once, the WIT meeting wasn't one man (me!) and fifty women, it was pretty much a 50/50 split. I got up and talked about the business case, why men are essential to gender equality and my journey. I asked for willing volunteers and by the end of the day, I had a dozen new allies.'

If you want to get men along to a women's event (and there are lots of good reasons that you should – men need to hear what women have to say a lot more), try to not have the word 'woman' in the event title. Clearly, this is not appropriate for things like International Women's Day, but phrasing the topic in a way designed to actively encourage men's attendance helps. Many have also renamed their women's networks as gender networks.

We also leveraged our internal networks, since you often find that people interested in inclusion locate each other across the organisation. Through our networks and the networks of other volunteers, we

swelled the ranks of volunteer allies. Finally, we identified sympathetic senior leaders and used them to
pass on the message and help gain recruits. There is
no denying that for any programme in a corporate
environment, getting senior sponsorship is critical,
even when we were senior leaders in our own right.

At this point, you might be thinking, 'Why not send a
broad email asking for volunteers or do more aggressive marketing to increase the numbers more quickly?'
The risk of getting too big too fast is that you can end
up with a lot of people signing up who think it is a
good idea but don't yet have a good understanding of the issues, and aren't committed to spending
enough time on it to make a discernible difference. A
male ally at another investment bank called these men
'Boy Scout Allies' – only there for the badge. We recommend trying a combination of approaches, because
there will be a lot of work to do.

Becoming informed

Once you have a team of committed volunteers,
what's next? We've found that you need to give
your allies a bit of time to develop their understanding of the subject. They need to build up expertise
because, make no mistake, this is going to be hard
work. Your allies will have to convince lots of other
men to take action. Some of these men genuinely
won't care, or won't want to give the time to make

changes. They will ask tough questions and have opinions that will need to be challenged, so equipping your allies with the knowledge to deal with a sceptical audience is key.

As a group, we sought out books, articles and TED Talks on gender bias and regularly shared these with each other. For the latter, we would often read or watch together and discuss as a group. We would set homework for the group to read or watch and compare notes later. We have featured some of the sources of information we found helpful in the Useful Resources section at the end of this book. Being well-read and familiar with research is important when talking to people inside the organisation, as it will show your interest and commitment to learning and so help you connect with other women and men interested in the topic. It can also be a useful recruiting tool for potential allies who are often interested to learn more but unsure of where to start.

Talking to women in the organisation

To be an effective ally you need to understand the biases, barriers and issues that women are facing in your organisation and where you can help. The best way to develop this understanding is by listening to the women around you in the organisation, in the media and at home. This may not be as easy as you might think. Often, women don't share this type of information unless they are asked, perhaps because they have just accepted the behaviour, they don't want to be perceived as complaining, or they believe that their issue is unique to their relationship with a particular person. This is why asking open questions and actively listening are so important to help make the invisible, visible to you.

It is critical that women in the company talk about their experiences, and that they feel safe to do so. When you first start discussing gender challenges with men, they will often say, 'This is old news, it doesn't happen anymore' or, 'That doesn't happen here.' Hearing stories about the recent experiences of women in your company is powerful and will make a real difference in changing mindsets.

Allies talking to women in the organisation is important for a number of other reasons. First, it helps to develop insight into the organisation and make it easier to see the kinds of behaviours to look out for. For example, if women find they aren't listened to at meetings, the organisation can create meeting guidelines and approaches which specifically challenge and improve on this type of behaviour.

Second, it improves allies' ability to talk to women in their organisation. Many men (including us – Gary and Stephen) aren't skilled at talking to women at work. It makes us feel uncomfortable, particularly when the women are in a different age range. Learning how to talk to women in a work environment is a key skill all allies will need, so it is important to develop it by practising.

Third, it can provide motivation. Speaking to women about gender balance can be helpful in convincing yourself and others of the need to work on this. If you find yourself thinking, 'Can I still commit enough time to this?' or, 'Is this really important?', talking to people about recent examples of the challenges they continue to face is a good source of motivation.

In this book we include a number of our stories, but it's important that you build your own sets of stories and anecdotes, as this is the most impactful way to win over people's hearts and minds.

Motivating men: ingredients for success

Having managed to get a group of men to an ally event, how do you keep them engaged? Here are four things worth considering:

1. **Get them talking.** Make sure that this is a dialogue where everyone's lived experience matters. A 'come sit with me' red chair event is a good start.[1] People take turns sitting on the chair and share a story personal to them, often on a theme linked to gender equality. Sharing experience like this begins to break down barriers. It will unearth stories that are deeply personal

and often very touching. We highly recommend running these kinds of events.

2. **Make it fun and interactive.** The events in the following videos/articles are easy to set up, and have proven to be fun and to get people talking to others that they might not normally interact with:

   - TV 2/All that we share[2]

   - Life of privilege explained in a $100 race[3]

   - Throwing paper balls into a bin[4]

3. **Talk about the negative impact on men.** There are lots of articles, studies and TED Talks that make it clear that gender equality is good for everyone. There is also research showing the price men can pay, both physically and mentally, when trying to live up to male stereotypes. For example, a Catalyst report talks about the pressure men face to always be a winner, to not show emotion or weakness, to be a 'man's man'.[5] Getting men to open up and explore how they feel about their health and their mental wellbeing can be powerful. It is a starting point for a conversation and maybe, by showing a little bit of vulnerability, they can become more active in listening to the daily concerns of people around them, especially their female colleagues.

4. **Talk about the benefits for men.** One thing we've learned from speaking to men is that a number of the benefits and policies that can be assumed to be primarily for women, such as parenting

leave and flexible working, are also valued by men. Yet, men are more reluctant to use these policies than women. Highlighting examples of senior men taking advantage of these policies encourages other men to use them. The Covid-19 situation is another good example of the power of role models. In many knowledge-based firms, senior leaders and managers were forced to work (effectively) from home for many months. This changed how many organisations will think about working from home and whether it is necessary for all staff to be in the office full-time.

Don't forget the business case

Many people actively working on workplace gender equality advise starting with the business case. Some of the key benefits and research in this regard are:

- **Improved profit.** Companies in the top quartile for gender diversity are 15% more likely to have financial returns above their respective national industry medians.[6]

- **Greater innovation.** Teams comprised both men and women produce 26% higher patent citation rates than the norm.[7]

- **An engaged and motivated workforce.** Diverse and more inclusive workforces demonstrate more collaboration (1.5x), greater team commitment (1.4x) and more discretionary effort (1.1x).[8]

- **Products for all genders.** When first deployed, airbags killed women and children.[9] Similar challenges were seen with police protective clothing[10] and the design of the personal protective equipment (PPE) used in the recent Covid-19 pandemic.[11]

- **Unbiased products.** When the Apple Watch launched in 2014, it was widely reported as 'designed by men, for men' and lacking key features that women would expect for health tracking.[12] When Goldman Sachs launched a new Apple Pay card service, a number of people reported that credit limits were different for men and women even when they had identical credit scores.[13]

All in all, it is easy to paint a compelling picture for the men in the room as to why diversity and inclusion should matter to them and their teams; why it matters to the organisation, why it should matter to their family and everyone around them, and why it will matter to every company they work for in the future. In addition, increasing their knowledge on the subject positions them to improve their own career outcomes.

Our experience talking to men

We (Stephen, Gary and Jill) and the teams we have worked with, have talked to thousands of men about gender equality at work. Here's a summary of what they tend to say:

- Most agree that gender diversity is an issue, especially in leadership roles.

- Men often do not recognise that their own biases and behaviours are part of the problem – it is usually other people's biases that are seen as the issue.

- Men struggle to identify what they can do to make a difference or are too afraid of making a mistake and doing or saying the wrong thing to help.

- Where men say they are willing to help, they often don't follow through.

- Men in particular have a low bar for measuring success. They will often highlight 'I hired a woman recently' as evidence of progress.

There are a number of themes that come up again and again. Below are some of the main points men make, what we think these mean and how we respond.

'I treat everyone fairly and equally'

It is likely that the person saying this is open to having a dialogue so you don't want to alienate them straight away by disagreeing with them. Initially, treating everyone fairly and equally seems a laudable objective. But treating people equally is often understood to mean treating people the same. While you want to give everyone in your team access to the same level of support and similar opportunities, it is almost impossible, and in fact not helpful if you intend to achieve *equitable outcomes*, to treat them all the same.

An easy way to think of it is that treating everyone the same is like making everyone wear unisex clothing. You can't take a one size fits all approach to managing different genders and ethnicities any more than you can make one type of clothing that works for everyone. Often, it means you treat everyone like they are men – which is also how unisex clothing is designed, you'll rarely see unisex clothing designed with the female form in mind.

'I always hire the best person for the job'

When we encounter this, our response is, 'The company is not asking you to hire the best person for the job. We are asking you to hire the best person for your team or for the company. If your team is made up of eight white men, it is unlikely that another one will be the best person for your team.' This is often followed by a comment along the lines of, 'If I have two identical candidates, one male, one female are you asking me to always hire the woman?' To which we say, 'That never happens. You never have two identical candidates of different genders or ethnicity, so the example isn't realistic. Putting that to one side though, if it did happen that you had two equally qualified candidates, we would recommend always hiring the candidate from a minority group as they are bringing something additional (their diversity) to your team.'

We would make a few additional notes on this advice. One, this viewpoint depends on you genuinely believing in the business case for greater diversity in teams. Two, if you just hire one woman into a team of eight men, the chances are that she might not find it the most inclusive experience so you may need to hire more women to join her. Three, 'merit' is a qualitative judgement so it's worth exploring what merit means in the particular context of a role and how people can demonstrate it. It's surprising just how seldom people question what merit means.

'No women apply for the jobs'/'It's a pipeline problem in our industry/sector/field'

In other words, 'It's somebody else's problem, not mine.' Focusing on the pipeline problem is a way of the manager avoiding accountability for improving the diversity of their team. There are many things that can be done to improve their chances of hiring more women. Better still, we would highlight examples of male leaders who have been successful in this.

The easiest way to start people in the right direction is to ask them to look at job descriptions. It comes as a surprise to most people (certainly most men) that the language they use in job descriptions and role definitions can put some people, especially women, off applying. We make some further practical suggestions on language in Chapter 5 on hiring and the language used in job descriptions is a simple thing that any hiring manager can do that can make a big difference. Another point we make is that often you'll find similar teams in the organisation who are having a lot more success hiring diverse candidates, so they should look at what this team is doing that they are not.

'I don't know what I can say anymore'

In our experience, when a man says this, it could be coming from a couple of different perspectives. One is in the 'political correctness gone mad' vein, where he believes that he has been victimised because someone else felt uncomfortable about something he said. The second is that he is genuinely unsure what words are deemed as inappropriate.

In the first case, it can take quite a long conversation to help someone understand that in an inclusive environment, it is often not about the intent of the speaker but the impact on the recipient of the language that is used. If what you say is making someone feel uncomfortable or like they do not belong, then you need to try and avoid using that language so that they can feel positively about being part of your team. Continued use of words that make them feel less welcome has a cumulative effect and over time will likely reduce their motivation and, hence, their performance in the team.

In both cases, it is worth making the point that no-one is perfect and it is easy for people to make mistakes and say the wrong thing – we all do it on occasion. It is important that you build an atmosphere where people feel comfortable pointing out non-inclusive language, and when you are picked up on it, you have to be willing to apologise and commit to try and do better next time. It is good to have honest conversations with your whole team about what language you agree is unacceptable and should be avoided.

'This problem will naturally disappear'/'Young people don't have these issues'

The younger generations are far more aware of gender equality than those who joined the workforce in the '70s, '80s and '90s. They are far more likely to have had mothers who worked while they were children and have seen more female role models in senior positions. They are also far more likely to have friends from a variety of diverse backgrounds. Yet, if we leave it to the next generation then a) we are going to be waiting an awfully long time for better gender balance in the workplace and b) we are not taking responsibility to deal with it. Also, we are not convinced that younger people will necessarily behave in a more inclusive way. Male feminists and anti-racists are not new phenomena. Moreover, gender stereotypes are still knitted into most cultures and are pretty hard to shift. If boys are steered towards different subjects to girls at schools, colleges and universities, then a lot of their formative experiences prior to entering the workforce may still be in male-dominated environments, which in turn can reinforce those same biases that we already see in men in the workforce.

When we ran our workshops, we found that younger men benefited just as much from the conversations and practical tips.

'Diversity has gone too far'/'There is too much positive discrimination'

From our experience, many people have, at some time, thought that a person was in a particular role or promoted to a certain level because of their gender or a combination of gender and ethnicity. A smaller group feel that there is now systematic positive discrimination (meaning favouring a group unfairly) in organisations and that the prospects of the majority in that organisation are harmed as a result. Our experience is that people don't generally air this opinion unless they feel that they are in an environment in which it is safe to share. In our workshop, we often try to provoke a discussion on this point as we know it's likely that some people will be thinking this but may not be willing to say it.

There are a few reasons we think some people have this opinion. First, most people don't understand the difference between positive action and positive discrimination. It is not something that is typically discussed in organisations so we shouldn't be surprised that it isn't well understood. Positive action is something many companies put in place to help under-represented groups overcome barriers and biases that the majority group does not experience. Positive action can take the form of networks for under-represented groups, leadership acceleration courses to help prepare them for promotion or a special focus on checking that diverse groups are adequately represented in the promotion process.

Organisations put these positive actions in place when diverse groups are either under-represented or disadvantaged in some way. The problem is that often this isn't clear to the majority because the reason for the positive action isn't highlighted. Few companies will admit to having biases and a culture in which minorities find it harder to be hired or promoted in the expected numbers. This situation leads to some employees wondering, 'Why am I not getting this special treatment?', which can underpin perceptions of positive discrimination.

Second, there is a small minority of managers who are unfairly favouring candidates who are members of minority groups. (We have noticed that it's mostly managers in the majority ethnic and gender groups who do this.) They are under pressure to improve the diversity of their departments and either don't have the knowledge and skills to do this effectively or are looking for a quick fix and so practise positive discrimination. It is hard to argue that this doesn't happen, so we tend to make the point that while you might know of an example, it happens infrequently and it is important not to exaggerate the impact.

Finally, as we discussed in Chapter 1, it can be down to poor communication or unthinking managers who have been asked to look at the diversity of promotion candidates and then tell others that they have been 'told to promote more women'.

'Lack of women in leadership is down to childcare'

It sometimes seems to us that every detailed conversation about gender balance in leadership ends up a discussion about childcare. It is a key concern and if the organisation does not have an inclusive approach and strong supporting policies for their employees who are, or want to be parents, we can see how it might be easy to reach this conclusion.

Our simple response to this (as with many other statements) is to ask if they can cite some research that has proved this to be true. As we have seen from the research we have shared in this book so far, there is ample evidence that plenty of other factors impact a woman's career progress beyond being a mother and childcare issues. For many women, this is not the main reason for their unequal representation in leadership roles. After all, not all women have/will have children and many of those who do will have supportive partners and/or face tough challenges balancing work and family life for a relatively short period of their careers.

That being said, organisations do need to have a strong, joined-up approach to parental leave and both men and women taking time out for career breaks, whether to have children or for other reasons.

'I've not seen any of these issues, I don't think there is a problem'

The first thing to point out to someone who says this is that men tend not to see many of the subtle ways in which women experience sexism. The evidence and reasons for this are discussed in Chapter 1. We also ask these men why they think this, and then explore the commentary from their colleagues telling them about the challenges they face. The second issue we discuss is the proportional representation of women in their teams and our view that a lack of women is an issue, even if they haven't seen poor behaviours. Our aim is to help them understand that many of the challenges faced by women are currently invisible to them and that conversations like these will help make them visible.

'I am not privileged'

Everyone has a different lived experience that shapes who they are. Some people have come from a disadvantaged background that resulted in fewer opportunities to access high-quality education, having a home life that made studying hard, or not being able to go on to higher education. Some might have had access to work experiences or job opportunities that others did not. We are not saying that all men have had a privileged upbringing or life. Our point is that the world of work has historically been shaped for men as the default; hence, as we have described in the section on bias in Chapter 1, there are specific expectations of how people behave and are recognised at work that are different for men and women.[14] For example, a lot of people still assume that men are more ambitious and women will sacrifice their careers to raise a family, despite research showing that this is no longer true.[15] Given that these expectations and practices have centred on men, they often have relative advantages in workplace settings and men historically have had access to opportunities that women have not, even without realising it.

This also means that women have to think about their gender in a workplace that has been designed for men, whereas men frequently do not. As a man, particularly in a male-dominated industry, it is rare that you will have to think about your gender. It is within this context that we say men have a privilege in the workplace compared to women.

'It's genetics, isn't it'

A few men out there believe there are genetic reasons why women are 'not cut out for' certain roles in the workplace. We haven't come across many men willing to voice this, though there have been a few well-publicised examples. On one occasion, when asked whether he thought there was a particular issue with gender diversity in technology, a man did suggest that it was 'all down to genetics' and that it had 'been proven' that women are not as skilled as men at the logical, structured thought processes required to make a strong software engineer. Before we could respond, most of the other men in the room jumped in to argue that this was patently not correct and that they had all known extremely talented female engineers.

We do have a response, though, in the form of an interesting case study that we have cited many times which strongly suggests that the belief that women are not as good as men at writing software is incorrect.[16]

CASE STUDY: GENDER DIFFERENCES AND BIAS IN OPEN SOURCE

A study comparing acceptance rates of contributions from men and women in an open-source software community found that, overall, women's contributions tend to be accepted more often than men's – but when a woman's gender is identifiable, they are rejected more frequently.

What is fascinating about this research is that they found that women were better at coding than men, but this was only acknowledged when the people assessing the code were not aware of the gender of the coder. This is especially surprising given that most software written today is written by men.

The study looked at open-source software and how often men and women's code changes were approved by the expert reviewers for that software, with approval of a change being a measure of the quality of that software change. The study further analysed whether the reviewer knew the gender of the coder and, when it was, whether that female coder was known to the reviewer or not.

The first finding was a bit of a surprise (at least, it was for a lot of men we knew working within the software industry). The approval rate of the changes submitted by women to the expert reviewers was 79%, and 75% for men, when the reviewers were not aware of the gender of the coder. This suggests that women were better/more successful at writing code than men, based on the fact that their contributions were more frequently accepted by a peer group of experts in that software product.

The second finding was not so surprising. When the approver knew the gender of the coder (and that person was not known to the approver), women's approval rates for submitted software changes dropped to 57%, whereas men's dropped to 62%, clearly demonstrating a bias against women.

The study's authors argue the data shows that, 'Women in open source are, on average, more competent than men and that discrimination against women does exist in open source.'

Things that might go wrong

In the course of setting up the allies group and talking to groups of men, we hit a few areas of resistance. We expect these issues may well be common so we have included tips to help the reader identify potential blockers.

First, when we started discussing a male allies network, a number of the women and Employee Resource Groups (ERGs) we worked with were a little wary or in some cases actively resistant, asking, 'Do we really need help on this? What do you know about the subject?' Don't be surprised if this happens. Our advice is to confess if you know little about the subject. Say that you are willing to learn and that you, as a man and a member of the majority group, can help by talking to other men and get that large population more motivated to act on diversity and inclusion. What worked for us was to keep explaining what we were doing, trying to show evidence where possible of how it was working and gradually, over time, these groups came to accept that our efforts were beneficial to diversity and inclusion initiatives.

Another frequently asked question was, 'Why do we need allies? Isn't this about unconscious bias? Shouldn't we provide unconscious bias training to everyone?' Unconscious bias training can help men and women alike understand their biases and how they might be affecting the day-to-day decisions they make, though research suggests that it does little to encourage people to take action to deal with these biases.[17] Allies need to be equipped with the knowledge, motivation and skills to help organisations take concrete steps to overcome these biases.

Key takeaways

It's not easy to involve men in actively acting as allies for gender inclusion. To help you, we have shared our learning about:

- How to get started with a steering group and a clear sense of purpose

- How to build a network of allies

- Ingredients for a well-motivated group, committed to the necessary chunk of time

- Challenges and questions you can expect and how to deal with them

The good news is, we have found men to be willing to discuss how to improve inclusion and gender equality, even those who are sceptical.

In the next chapter, we'll discuss some of the ways that the group can learn more about gender equality and some of the content and structure we've put in place to guide discussions, with the aim of sharing experiences and good practice for improving inclusion and addressing gender biases at work.

Chapter 3

Challenging Male Mindsets

After we'd pulled together a number of senior men to run our male allies steering committee and had begun to recruit men for our allies network, we needed to work out what to do next to help change the culture. In this chapter, we explain what we tried and learned that may help speed up the journey for you.

A workshop for allies

We decided to create a workshop with the aim of helping people better understand women's experiences at the firm. We started by reaching out to the mid- and junior-level women at our organisation and finding out what behaviours and assumptions teams and managers were making that made it more difficult for them to do their jobs and be successful (the kinds of issues we talked about in Chapter 1). This was precisely the feedback we needed to gain to get some momentum and start changing the minds and beliefs of the men around us.

But the workshop needed to be about more than just relaying the female experience; it had to be about what men could personally do to change and improve the situation. One of the challenges we found in previous attempts at inclusivity training was that it focused on unconscious bias which, although a useful first step in building understanding of the problem, often did not provide practical tips on what an individual could do differently.

We also wanted to give men a forum to express their views. Research shows that the male voice is missing from discussions on gender equality.[1] We had collated feedback from women but we also felt that men should be able to give their view. When we discussed what the women had told us, what did the men think and feel about it? Was it something they saw in their teams and, if so, did they have ideas on how to deal with it? Had they spoken up or intervened when their female colleagues had an issue?

Our final priority was to create something engaging for men. It had to be interactive and give everyone an opportunity to contribute. We didn't want to have men in the room hiding from the conversation.

We wanted to hear from all of them in as open and honest a conversation as possible. We took great pains to make sure it was never described as training; it would be a workshop where everyone got involved and was expected to arrive at their own action points.

At this point, we would like to make something clear. The company where we started our male allies' journey was, and still is, a tremendous company to work for. On the whole, we think it treats all of its workforce well and has put huge investment into building diversity and inclusion into the way it does business. Probably more so than many other employers. However, no company is perfect, because the individuals working there aren't perfect either. Pretty much every company has more to do.

As our experience of running these workshops has increased and we've worked with companies in other industries and with government bodies, we have found that many of the comments and experiences raised are shared across these different organisations. The challenges we've found are certainly not unique to the firm in which we built this programme.

Just for men?

We have run sessions just for men and sessions with a mix of men and women, each had their pluses and minuses. Involving women in the sessions provides valuable and sometimes unexpected perspectives.

For example, a great interaction occurred in one of the mixed sessions whereupon a man was heard to say, 'I find it really difficult to talk about this subject' and the woman next to him replied, 'Well, actually so do I.'

That was quite an eye-opener, even to us, because men tend to assume that women talk about this subject frequently and are comfortable with it. Men can also assume that if women aren't talking about these issues, it must mean there isn't a problem. There are many reasons why women might feel uncomfortable having this conversation, even among other women, and having it with men might be all the more difficult. For example, they may believe they are the only ones having difficulties, or don't want to risk accusations of being 'difficult' or not a team player. Women have told us it can be emotionally tiring and challenging to raise complaints and that they fear further jeopardising their career progress. Men hearing this perspective benefit from a valuable lesson on not making assumptions.

In the first couple of years, though, we focused on running the workshop with male participants. We wanted men to be completely open and honest and felt we needed to create a comfortable environment for them to share honestly what they were thinking, particularly if they were confused or uncertain about what was acceptable. We didn't want them to feel embarrassed, or that they needed to rein in what they were prepared to say in front of women. In particular, if they did feel that women's views about challenges they faced were unfounded, we needed to know about that so we could start having a conversation to tackle it.

It is, of course, important at all-male sessions that the point of view of female colleagues is represented. Involving women can be a challenge. Some, usually more senior women, are happy to talk about their experiences, but others find it emotionally draining and a potential risk to their reputation and career progress. These fears are not misplaced, according to recent academic research.[2] Nevertheless, we recommend finding a way to bring women's voices into the room, either physically (perhaps in a small group) or by summarising the feedback from female colleagues. Or even using short filmed interviews with women, perhaps including those who have recently left the organisation.

Over time, as our Male Allies group matured and became more accepted and understood, we started running more mixed sessions, although still with the majority of participants being male. A mixed session with equal numbers of men and women is a great follow-up to a male-only workshop.

One final point to highlight is that, when running all-male workshops, it's a great idea to let the women in the same teams know what's happening and why. After doing this, we found women to be extremely supportive and helpful with getting attendees. It's also a good idea to ask women whether they see changes after workshops have been run, although change does take time and continual reminders.

Mandatory attendance?

Our next debate was whether we should make attendance mandatory or voluntary. On one hand, studies have shown that mandatory diversity and inclusion training does not work and can create a backlash.[3] On the other hand, making attendance voluntary risks attracting only those who are already convinced of the importance of diversity and inclusion.

Based on our experience, for anyone considering rolling out a similar programme, we would recommend two things. First, align the workshop to an overall diversity and inclusion package of learning. Second, make it mandatory for all staff to attend a certain amount of diversity and inclusion learning and/or events each year, but allow them to choose which ones.

The other thing we learned that was incredibly useful from the start was to have two presenters. If there was one person on their own and the atmosphere in the room got a little abrasive, it became difficult to stay on message and deal with the most divisive voices. A second person can read the room and step in if things get challenging, as well as identify the quieter voices and encourage them to get involved.

Workshop content

Next, we want to look at how to run the workshop. It is important to set the right tone from the beginning of the workshop. We say something like:

'This is not about making anyone feel guilty and it is not anybody's fault. We are all products of our own cultural upbringing and the biases in the media, so it is understandable that people come to work with learned biases and behaviours. You're not here because someone has spotted you doing or saying something wrong. No-one comes into work intending to be deliberately unkind, but sometimes people get into ways of working that are not supportive of gender equality. By working together, we can challenge these behaviours and improve the culture.

'Our company has a strong track record of supporting diversity and inclusion but more progress is needed. It is not enough to hire and promote more women, we also need to ensure that they are motivated to stay with the company. This does require the company to have the right policies and procedures to help us, but it is down to all of us as individuals to make everyone feel they belong. We are going to share plenty of practical tips on how best to do that. Most importantly, we want to hear from you and get your ideas and perspectives on things that we can all do better.'

When we run these groups, in the last part of the introduction, we tell our stories about why we are there, why we got involved and what it has taught us. The same stories that we shared in the introduction to the book.

Asking what men think

The next stage is to get people involved. We ask everyone to introduce themselves, who they are and what they do, and to answer the question, 'Is there a diversity problem in your area?' and share any stories of what they've seen.

It is important that everyone has that initial opportunity to participate. As we said earlier, we don't want anyone to hide and we need to understand where each of them is on their personal journey. We have found this ranges from complete ignorance and lack of interest, or even mild hostility, through to being an enthusiastic supporter, with the middle ground of being aware but not motivated to take action. This debate usually establishes some hot topics and key areas for discussion.

Starting in this way also allows us to establish credibility and demonstrate some expertise. For instance, when men have complained about the lack of a female pipeline, we talk about the research that shows how women don't apply to jobs with long lists of skills unless they feel they have all of them (whereas men will apply if they have just 60%) and suggest that they could easily do something about that by writing better role descriptions.[4]

The goal at this stage is to get people talking, try not to make any judgements and just listen to what they have to say. We take notes to help guide the conversation later and thank participants for their honesty.

Male privilege

Now that everybody has had an opportunity to contribute, we like to dial it up a little, so we show the TED Talk by the American writer and sociologist, Dr Michael Kimmel, entitled 'Why gender equality is good for everyone – men included'.[5]

This talk tends to give people the opportunity to reconsider things men commonly believe, such as that they always treat people fairly and equally. The Kimmel video usually has a real impact on the attendees as he tells the audience why he got involved in gender equality and why they should too. It has some clear messages about male privilege, particularly white male privilege, and explains how that privilege is often invisible to those who have it. It is not only about male privilege, but also demonstrates the different lived experiences between women, for example, the difference between the experience of a white woman and a black woman, and how a white woman won't have to think about race in the way a black woman does.

The talk usually gets quite a reaction from the audience. It contains some good stories and anecdotes, quite a lot of humour and generates lots of good material to bring into the workshop discussion.

When the video is over, we ask the men in the room, 'What do you think? Did those messages resonate? Was there anything that changed your perspective? Anything you particularly liked or enjoyed?' In the discussion that follows, we make sure that the below points are well understood:

- That there is continuous and inherent bias against women in the workplace

- That privilege is invisible to those who have it

- That men have been beneficiaries of this privilege and it has been continuously reinforced throughout history

- That to men, and particularly white men, race and gender is often invisible, as they don't need to think about it; and that to improve gender equality they need to work on their perception

- That gender equality is beneficial to men and especially to the way that men are now saying they want to live their lives

The message around privilege usually hits home, especially the fact that, even though we all have different backgrounds and face different challenges, men make assumptions about entitlement that they may never have realised before. Occasionally, men take exception to the suggestion that they are privileged. Often, this is because they have had a challenging upbringing and so feel offended by the suggestion that they have had privileges that others haven't. We included our suggested responses to this in the previous chapter.

If the concept of male privilege is providing difficult to convey, we have another suggestion. An excellent blog about inclusive leadership from Royal Navy Captain Steve Prest (@fightingsailor) uses the term 'relative advantage'. He also makes good use of an analogy about a game of table football on an uneven floor that requires one team to shoot uphill.[6]

Biases and behaviours

A large section of our workshop is then taken up with walking through the biases and behaviours that we have collated from our discussions with the women in the organisation. The 5Cs from Chapter 1 can be tailored to suit the issues women report in their organisation. For our firm, we organised the issues into four main themes, which we present in our workshop using a series of 'bias explored' slides with quotes from female colleagues. The themes are:

- Women aren't subject matter experts/technical
- Women aren't committed to their careers
- Women like administrative tasks
- It is easier to be promoted as a woman

We give the attendees a few minutes to read each slide with the quotes and then we prompt conversation with a series of questions, such as:

- Does this resonate with your experience?
- Have you seen this happening in your team?
- If you have, how did you deal with it?
- Do you have some ideas of what good practices we could employ to minimise this happening?

We then move on to behaviours, taking a similar approach and covering issues such as:

- Men commenting about women who walk past
- Women feeling ignored, silenced or left out of conversations

- Women receiving a less enthusiastic greeting from the team than their male colleagues

- Social events that exclude certain populations, particularly events focused around sport or drinking

- Comments suggesting women are overly focused on form over function

- Reinforcing stereotypes through comments such as, 'That was a blonde moment'

- Using phrases like 'Come on ladies' to a group of men, or 'You need to man up', 'He took it like a man' and, 'She needs to grow a pair'

- Referring to a woman as a girl, implying immaturity

- Interrupting or talking over others

Practical tips

A key part of the workshop is providing some practical tips, as it has to be about more than just understanding the problem. We want men to leave with fresh ideas and, importantly, we are always keen to hear their ideas – and we have heard many. We have pulled together these ideas in the next few chapters.

We finish up with a few minutes of reflection on what we have discussed and then ask them to write down one or two things that they are going to do differently.

The outcomes: evidence of success

Overall, over more than four years, our core Male Allies group of around ten or fifteen men have put in thousands of hours persuading our colleagues to make changes to how they behave at work. We have run this workshop with over 2,000 men in leadership positions in multiple locations – in London, Bournemouth and Glasgow in the UK; in Mumbai, Hyderabad and Bangalore in India; in Singapore and Buenos Aires; and in New York, Jersey City, Brooklyn, Houston, Chicago, Dallas and Tampa in the US. We wanted them to help improve the workplace culture for everyone, not just female colleagues. Was it worth it? Did we succeed? If so, how would we know?

Measuring inclusion

The best way to assess the impact of running workshops is to regularly measure inclusion. This will show whether improvements in inclusion correlate with the number of workshops attended in an office, team or department. Measuring inclusion isn't as easy as measuring representation and often gets less focus in organisations. Inclusion is best measured through anonymous employee surveys that ask questions about how employees feel about the organisation, their managers and promotion opportunities, and questions that capture information about their gender, race, location and level in the organisation. Once you have implemented new behaviours, for example by explaining how to run more inclusive meetings or how to call out accidental bias when you see it, we recommend you measure behavioural change, because changes in attitudes often follow changes in behaviour. The surveys need to be regular, at least yearly, and with as much consistency as possible in the questions asked, to enable like-for-like comparisons that allow progress to be assessed. Alongside employee surveys, other measures, such as levels of attendance at diversity and inclusion events, or amount of inclusion-related training completed, can also be used.

In our case, inclusion wasn't being measured frequently or consistently enough to use as benchmark. Nevertheless, there were indicators that could tell us whether we were making a difference. Let's start with the workshop.

Evaluating the workshop

Our stated intent for our male allies workshop was:

1. To increase awareness and understanding of diversity and inclusion in the workplace

2. To have in-depth discussions about real examples of where unconscious and conscious biases and a lack of inclusivity had impacted people within the firm

3. To identify specific actions and best practices that managers could take back to their teams

4. To recruit new members to our network and get their commitment to ongoing participation

The feedback from attendees showed that we achieved the first two objectives. Most sessions scored an overall satisfaction rating of around 4.5 out of 5. The feedback revealed that the most valuable parts of the sessions were the examples of biases and behaviours that were causing problems, both the examples included in the workshop material and the anecdotes shared by the presenters and attendees. People found these useful in understanding the issues being discussed. Attendees also liked the interactivity of the sessions.

On objective three, we were particularly pleased with the number of ideas that came from participants. Over the next few chapters, we will go through some practical tips, many of which came from our workshop attendees and the ideas that they shared or co-created with us in the sessions.

None of these findings, though, proved that cultural change was happening. With regard to objective four, there were a few signs that things were changing. Pretty much everyone who attended signed up to our mailing list and we began to see more men at our women's diversity events and mental health awareness sessions.

We saw more men stepping forward as role models for flexible or dynamic working, and championing women's history month or joining cross-networking sessions across all of our Employee Resource Groups. We saw men embracing difficult conversations with women as part of our diversity dialogues series, a new set of workshops designed for men and women to discuss gender ideas together. We even saw several men come to our workshops more than once, when they wanted a refresher session or to find out if there was fresh research or new tips that we were promoting. Having people attend multiple sessions is unusual; we weren't seeing this with other forms of training.

After we had run workshops with more than 200 participants, we conducted a retrospective with our core male allies and the wider women's group that we supported. Using the quotes, biases and behaviours that we had collated from our early sessions with the women's group, we ran an interactive session to evaluate whether they were still seeing these or if they felt that there was evidence of things improving. The clear feedback from the session was that, in teams with a high attendance rate, instances of these kinds of behaviours had dramatically decreased and examples were much harder to find. There were one or two quite subtle biases that had been observed, but in the main, everyone felt that things were changing significantly for the better.

Success stories

Above all, the personal success stories that we hear give us the most satisfaction. We'd like to share a few here.

About six months into our allies journey, a diversity and inclusion fair took place in one of our offices. The Male Allies stand was positioned next to the WIT stand. We were chatting to one of the local women's network leads when she stopped and said, pointing to a man close by, 'If you could get him along to one of your workshops and change the way he operates, you would be doing everyone a favour.' Challenge accepted! She invited him over, we discussed what our Male Allies programme was about, he explained his rather robust opinions on the women's group and why there were so few women in technology and we agreed to continue the conversation at one of our workshops.

A couple of weeks later, he came along to a workshop and shared his thoughts further. He explained how he was 'pro-women', but that they needed to 'toughen up' to be successful in the technology field, to be more thick skinned and stand up for themselves. He thought women needed to adjust their behaviour to fit. A couple of hours later, he came up to us and said, 'Thank you for that session. It has given me a lot to think about. Perhaps I need to change how I go about things.' He went on to become a strong advocate for the programme.

Our second story is from when we visited one of our company's locations in India. We spoke to a woman who led the women's group in our infrastructure engineering team. This group had even lower female numbers than other technology groups which was something she was keen to address.

She spoke about how difficult it had been, a year earlier, for women working in the infrastructure department. They were often not included in social events, were mocked as the 'diversity hire' and frequently not given opportunities to demonstrate their technical skills. Morale among the women in the team was at an all-time low. As part of our global Male Allies programme, they decided to set up a local group specifically for the infrastructure team, created a strategy which they thought would work for them locally and got on and implemented it. The Male Allies group joined forces with the women's group and co-authored and sponsored a series of social events, networking sessions and technical learning sessions. The results were transformative.

Her experience a year on was that it was like working in a new department. All of the women in the team now felt engaged, listened to and respected, and the men around them were far more energised and involved. She felt it was down to the collaboration between the male allies and the women's group they supported.

Our final story comes from a man who was probably one of our most senior attendees. We have had several managing directors from the company attend our workshops, but few who were as senior as him. A couple of his direct reports had attended previously and had recommended the sessions to him. When we went round the group asking for initial views on the subject, he told his story.

He talked about how he had always considered himself to be an inclusive and decent leader who valued diverse opinions, but had come to realise that he must be doing something wrong. His current leadership had just one woman in a group of around ten and she was about to take a role elsewhere (a move that he actively supported) which meant that he would have a male-only leadership team. He said, 'I have to change. I can't keep doing the same thing, because I am likely to get the same outcome. I've come here today to get some ideas on what I can do differently.'

About two weeks later, he called to tell us how powerful he had found the workshop, how much he had reflected on what he had learned, and to share his new strategy for building a more diverse team. That someone in a senior position of influence has developed an approach to hire and promote more women into his team is one of our biggest success stories.

Gaining momentum

We started our programme by developing a session for the technology division of our company in the UK. Over the years, we found that the issues and themes were similar in many different places. The material worked well in the US, India and China, and in other business areas in the firm, such as operations and investment banking. It worked well in other industries, and we have used the workshop to help other firms get started on their journey. This broad applicability and interest is one of the reasons we decided to write this book. We have also learned how important it is to continually evolve the workshops to improve them and make them easier to run, ensuring their continued relevance to different audiences. What's more, we don't need to have all the answers because participants educate each other and are often more influential than the moderators in persuading other men of the need to change to tackle accidental gender bias.

After the workshop

After attending a workshop, many men want to take the conversation further. One of the follow-up ideas we had was to set up what we call diversity dialogues. In these sessions, a group of men and women discuss difficult questions about how men and women work together, questions that people can otherwise be too uncomfortable to ask and have an honest conversation about. Questions like, 'Do you treat your female staff differently to your male staff and, if so, how?' or, 'Is there an old boy's network inside the company?' or, 'What are the challenges a woman faces during the menopause?'

These conversations often yielded a number of actions and follow-ups, but simply having the conversation was important because it increased the shared understanding between men and women in the company. With practice, the team began to get better at these conversations and feel more comfortable discussing difficult topics more openly.

At the heart of an inclusive culture is the ability to create the safety and trust needed for people to have what they see as difficult conversations. Not just conversations about gender, or race or sexuality, but any topic people struggle to discuss with their colleagues. It could be a conversation about disability, mental health or simply asking how someone is after a life-impacting event (eg the death of a close family member). Our diversity dialogues were simply a way of helping people have these difficult discussions in a safe environment.

Organisations must give their employees the opportunity to continue these discussions. This requires not only additional resources being provided or focus groups set up, but also encouraging managers to give their employees time to engage in this learning.

Key takeaways

Running a well-designed workshop programme with men has a demonstrable effect on changing workplace culture to be more inclusive. This chapter has provided practical tips on why and how to implement such a programme, including:

- Why a workshop?

- The rationale for male-only sessions

- How to include women's voices

- Tips on content

- Evidence of success

In the next few chapters, we explore in detail the practical tips that we give in our workshops. The next chapter looks at how individuals can change their behaviour to avoid the negative outcomes of subtle, accidental bias.

Chapter 4

Tackling Bias To Build Inclusive Teams

Now you have engaged the support of male allies, what do you want them to do? Inclusive cultures will not simply appear once there is better understanding of the challenges faced by women and minority groups. We can all do something differently. This chapter suggests how, both individually and working together in teams, we can challenge unhelpful aspects of workplace culture to make the most of individual talent and do our best to ensure everyone can feel a sense of belonging. The practical advice given is as relevant to our female readers as male readers because anyone can be accidentally sexist and anyone can act as an ally.

Allies as agents of change

It is people who create the culture of their workplaces; not just leaders, everyone. Men, in particular, have an important role to play. This may seem unfair to women but there is power in men talking to men about accidentally sexist behaviour and ways to avoid this trap. This power comes from three things. First, the fact that men currently occupy more of the positions of power in many workplaces. Second, it can be more surprising, and thus impactful, to hear about what has long been thought of as a 'women's issue' from a man. Third, the more members of the dominant group are seen to take action, the more other members of that group will join in.

Striking the right tone is important. Changing the culture needs committed action from leaders and changes to systems and processes, which we discuss in later chapters. That said, there are also important changes that individuals can make.

An ally has to be a visible agent of change. Change can be driven by making gender visible. It is important that you look for and speak up about non-inclusive behaviours and attitudes. This chapter draws from good practice and good ideas suggested by men and women who have attended our workshops, to provide practical tips for individuals and teams.

Tips for individuals and teams

We've structured our tips around the 5Cs introduced in Chapter 1. We offer advice about what behaviour to call out, how to call it out and, importantly, we finish this chapter with advice on what to say and do if you find *yourself* being called out for accidentally sexist behaviour.

Our advice is given in the spirit of allies taking responsibility for stepping in when women (including women who are also members of other minority groups) experience challenges. It's much more effective and less emotionally draining for an ally to intervene than for the person concerned to challenge the behaviour of others or raise a grievance. When you call something out, it helps reinforce to others that it is OK to speak up. You may even find the person making the comment is grateful for being called out on it. Most people don't make sexist comments intentionally and while often they realise they've said something inappropriate they can be unsure how to remedy it, so this gives them a chance to apologise at the time.

Capability

A common frustration expressed by women is when managers or colleagues routinely expect them to pick up administration tasks such as taking meeting minutes, organising leaving cards and presents or social events, and generally be 'helpful' to colleagues, rather than being given work that builds their profile. This is driven by the stereotypical view of 'women's work': that women are good at admin and managing relationships, and have good attention to detail. Stephen discusses one of the ways he caught himself gender stereotyping:

> 'I sometimes have to go on the trading floor of the investment bank, where the floors are huge and I often don't know where the person I'm looking for is sitting. I used to look around for a woman to ask for directions. I never thought about it at the time but I was unconsciously assuming they would be an administrative assistant and so might help me. I later realised the admin assistants sat near the offices at the back of the floors and so it's likely that I was bothering the female traders. I also realised there wouldn't need to be too many idiots like me in the firm to provide a constant stream of interruptions for the female traders on the floor. Now, I ask someone I know, or a man.'

Companies sometimes have additional projects or assignments, unrelated to people's core work, where volunteers often work beyond their normal hours to deliver. All too often, we see managers assigning female members of their team to engagement or diversity initiatives and male members to the innovation projects.

Women have this bias too. Research has shown that women are far more likely to volunteer for tasks that are not part of their core duties or are not likely to be rewarded or compensated for.[1] We are sure many of you will recognise this scenario. It's the weekly staff meeting and the boss has just asked if anyone would like to put their name forward for the latest HR initiative (eg mentoring, networking, recruitment, etc). Everyone looks down at their hands, avoiding eye contact. After a few moments of awkward silence, a woman in the room will usually step forward and volunteer.

The same bias can be seen in the allocation of stretch assignments or opportunities. Research has shown that men are more often evaluated on their potential and are less often required to prove their competence than women.[2] Also, the people you feel you know better are more likely to spring to mind for a task. This means that stretch and prestigious projects – which are taken into account when people are being judged 'on merit' for promotion – are more likely to be given to men and/or people in your 'clique'.

Our advice to managers is to stop and think about why you are selecting a man or a woman for a particular task and avoid stereotyping. Do the same for the provision of training, facilitating attendance at and travel to conferences, or when nominating people for committees or stretch activities and other things that help your team develop. Consider the diversity of the people to whom you are offering these opportunities, especially the more technical tasks. Better still, keep a record of who gets each type of task or learning opportunity as they arise, so you can be more even-handed in your allocation of tasks that allow people to develop or show their skills. Or, in project-based occupations such as professional services, hire a work allocation manager.

Constraints

Double standards

In Chapter 1, we presented evidence that accidental bias results in women being judged according to a double standard. For example, behaviour that in women – and in particular black women – is labelled as aggressive, but when displayed by a man is more likely to be described as passionate, assertive or ambitious.[3] A famous example of this is the negative press reaction to champion tennis player Serena Williams's assertion that the umpire in one of her US Open matches had treated her more harshly than the male players by applying the rules more strictly and deducting a game from her. Williams was supported in her claim by men and women on the tennis tour and some senior tennis officials.[4]

Academic researchers have studied the language used in written and verbal assessments of male and female staff and have found that the language used is different, and that the words used to describe men fit more closely with the qualities associated with leadership.[5,6,7] Examples include:

Describing Women	Describing Men
Good team player	Rising star
Conscientious	Skilled
Good attention to detail	Gets the job done
Helpful	Charismatic
Pleasant	Ambitious
Emotional	Passionate
Difficult	Maverick
Aggressive	Assertive

When you know this, especially as a man, you can explain how particular words can be interpreted in a way that gives men an advantage or disadvantages women. You can avoid misinterpretation by saying things like, 'She is appropriately assertive.' You can challenge other men by asking, 'Would you have used the same words to describe a man?' You can look at written assessments side by side and challenge any gender bias you notice.

This is important because every assessment contributes to who is considered the best person to promote 'on merit'.

Benevolent sexism

To remind you, benevolent sexism is when you make well-intentioned decisions about a woman's workload, her ability to take up a foreign posting, changes to her role on return from maternity leave, or which client she might find difficult, and so on, without asking the woman in question.

Here are a couple of examples that have come up in our workshops. Instances are usually (but not always) related to assumptions about women with children wanting to balance their personal and working lives.

Our first example was described by a female developer who was working on a large important programme that hit some major problems in testing shortly before a go live date. The team manager decided that the only way to get everything back on track was to get the whole team to work a couple of weekends to catch up. Except it wasn't quite the whole team. The manager simply assumed that the female developer in the team would have personal matters to attend to and did not invite her to take part. She found out about it after the first weekend when a team member asked her where she'd been. She might indeed have had personal commitments (as might male members of the team have had) but to not even be asked would hardly make that woman feel like a fully fledged member of the team.

Another example was when a senior manager was looking for someone in the UK to run a newly formed technical support team in Mumbai. He asked his female lead whether she could think of anyone suitable for the post. 'What about me?' she asked. 'I assumed that with a young family, you would not be willing to go,' he replied.

A long conversation resulted in this woman heading out to India for one of the most enjoyable and best learning experiences of her career. But it could easily have not happened if she had not pointed out the incorrect assumptions of her manager.

Managers can avoid these situations by asking women what their short- and long-term ambitions are and whether now is the right time for the opportunity in question. Sometimes male managers are hesitant about asking questions that touch on the personal circumstances of their employees, not wanting to 'over-step the mark'. It is fair to say that this must be approached sensitively and may require some open questions – asking personal questions out of context should certainly be avoided.

Over time, a manager should look to build trust with all their staff, get to know their personal circumstances and lived experience so that they can be comfortable asking questions about their employees' lives outside of work. The better they understand their team members, the more likely they are to identify the right opportunities, the right development actions and the right motivations to make their work lives much happier.

One of the results of the Covid-19 pandemic was that managers got to know the personal circumstances of their employees a lot better. As was widely reported, people got to see their colleagues' families, pets and homes – it made the world of work a little more human, which can't be a bad thing.

Connections

The importance of strong networks and friendly relationships with colleagues should not be underestimated. These connections help you feel that you 'fit in', stay up to date with what's going on and allow you to discuss work-related issues and relationships. Networks provide you with mentors who encourage you and sponsors who actively advocate for your career progress when you are not in the room. Yet, social connections and networks are not often talked about in relation to inclusion and feelings of belonging. We intend to put that right.

Informal social networking

Our biases can lead to different responses to colleagues in social situations at work. One interesting piece of research found that, 'Minorities simply had less interaction with [more] biased managers during their shifts.' It seems that managers didn't pay as much attention to them. This research found that individuals with implicit biases toward a group are less likely to speak to, more hesitant in speaking to, and less friendly toward group members. The impacts were less time spent managing them and a drop in employee productivity.[8]

Based on the feedback we received from our female colleagues, it seems that for some managers this hesitancy also applies to interactions with women. The women we spoke to felt ignored ('I feel like when I go over to speak to him, I'm just having a conversation with the back of his head'), left out of conversations, silenced, or that they weren't greeted with the same level of enthusiasm as men.

We recognise that this is tricky. For some men (and women, too), social conversations are difficult and it is easy to fall back on a comfort zone of safe conversations with people you know well. But if you find yourself starting every Monday morning in the office wandering over to the same bloke to have the same conversation about what happened in the football over the weekend, something needs to change.

Women too can limit their contacts by talking mainly to other women. After thinking about this, Jill said:

> 'I noticed that whenever I was invited to a conference or somewhere new to talk about gender equality in the workplace, I would invariably get a coffee and go and introduce myself to a woman or group of women. I guess that just felt more comfortable. I did the same

at social events where I didn't know many people. Now I introduce myself to more men.'

It does take a little bravery to start a conversation with someone you don't know well, but if you find out a bit more about them, next time you can include them in the conversation more easily. Allies should continuously look for opportunities to include, especially in social situations. Allies who manage teams should keep an eye out for in-groups and out-groups within their teams and work to bring the whole group together where possible. Attending diversity events and learning more about gender inclusion makes it feel easier and more comfortable to talk to people of another gender.

Many of us find networking hard and don't deliberately exclude people. It happens when we aren't paying attention to our tendency to gravitate to those who seem more like us. Addressing these issues often doesn't come naturally to people, but we have a few ideas that have been suggested by participants in our workshops. These ideas apply to managers of teams but many can be acted on by individual allies:

- **Hosts:** Every team has someone who is great at meeting new people. Make them 'hosts' who are charged with helping others to mix with people they don't often work with or don't know at all. Do this at client drinks, the Christmas party or a breakfast briefing – wherever.

- **'Outside the box' meetings:** Make opportunities to meet new people by inviting someone from outside your team to a meeting such as a problem-solving or idea generation session.

- **Coffee conversations:** Give everyone 'permission' to get to know more people at work. For example, suggest one day a week when people are expected to ask someone they don't know – ideally of a different gender – to have coffee with them. Or play lunch roulette, where people are matched with members of other teams. For team-mates in different physical locations, encourage virtual get-to-know sessions across geographies.

- **Lunch or breakfast:** Create social spaces for people to eat together.

- **Ten in ten:** Task new team members with having coffee with ten people they don't know in their first ten weeks.

- **Not the usual suspects:** Take someone different (ideally someone more junior) to a business development meeting, conference or client event, and be clear about their role there.

Work social events

Non-inclusive work practices can find their way into social events outside the workplace. If a manager's idea of team-building is drinks in the pub on a Friday evening, then the chances are that someone in the team is being excluded. Similarly, social events organised around football, golf and other sporting activities are unlikely to be embraced by everyone, regardless of gender. Many female sports fans complain about the assumption that they are less interested in sport than the blokes which means they are not invited to watch professional sports events. There are fewer opportunities for women to play sport with colleagues (such as in five-a-side football teams, golf or cycling sportives) because data shows that fewer women than men participate in these sports. Even when women do play or ride they rarely do so in gender mixed teams and we have heard many reports that women are rarely invited by their male colleagues to participate. This leaves women with fewer opportunities to get to know people from other teams in the organisation or their more senior colleagues.

This isn't to say you shouldn't have events organised around sport or eating and drinking; these types of events can play an important role in team development. However, you shouldn't have them all the time and they shouldn't be the *only* events you enjoy as a team. Variety is key. We suggest you create a diverse organising committee to run different types of social and / or networking events. With the increased demand for flexible working, it's important these events aren't always at the same time of day – as well as evening, think about a lunchtime or even a breakfast session. This should mean that, although not everyone will be able to make every event, everyone should be able to make some of them. And hopefully, a few of those women who were maybe thinking about moving on, might feel inclined to stay. You might even pick up a few opening conversational gambits to avoid those difficult social conversations on a Monday morning.

Credit

He-peating

Research has shown that a common occurrence is for a woman's idea to be ignored in a meeting and is then reintroduced by a man, at which point it is acknowledged; this phenomenon has been termed 'he-peating'.[9] If this occurs, it is important that whoever is chairing the meeting spots this and re-attributes the idea to the woman who first suggested it. Allies can also be ready to step in when the chair does not notice that the originator of an idea has not been credited, or in a less formal meeting with no chair.

Tips for what to say when you spot this include:

- 'Liz's point [repeat verbatim] is well taken because…'

- 'Thanks, David, that point builds on something that Samira was saying earlier. Samira, would you like to say more?'

- 'Thanks, David for bringing back up the good point that Samira made earlier.'

When someone's point seems to have been misunderstood, try:

- 'What I understood by Ella's point is...'
- 'It seems like we have different views about Ella's point. I think...'

We are suggesting specific language to help, although we expect people to find phrases that suit their personal style.

The chair, or individuals acting as allies, should make a point of asking for the opinions of team members who are less vocal in meetings. Recognise, though, that some people are not comfortable voicing their opinions in groups, or may need to reflect on what has been said before forming a view. In these cases, it is worth following up with those people so that they can share their thoughts after the meeting.

In general, crediting and praising each other's work or ideas is great practice. All people like to hear positive feedback.

Communication

Hear her

Research shows that women are interrupted far more often than men and that they struggle to have their voices heard.[10,11] We've also heard examples of women chairing a meeting, only to have a man step in and take over.

The first step for anyone who is chairing a meeting, especially a manager chairing a meeting of their team, is to observe who is talking and who is staying quiet. Look out for interruptions and gently bring the original speaker back into the conversation.

You could do this by saying something like, 'Can I stop you there? I will come back to you later. Mahmood, you were saying...'

When you do not have the power of being chair, a helpful tactic is to team up with a colleague to watch your back in meetings. It's far more comfortable for many to intervene on a colleague's behalf than to call out their own interrupter. Of course, if you feel comfortable enough to do this yourself, go ahead. Kamala Harris, US Vice President, deftly fended off interruptions during the 2020 election campaign by holding up her hand and saying, 'I'm speaking.'

Other ideas for what to say include:

- 'Andrew, I hadn't quite finished' or, 'If you could just hold that thought until I have finished.'

Some ideas for what to say on behalf of a colleague include:

- 'Jen, it sounds like you had more to say. Please, continue.'

- 'This is Jen's area/project. Would you like to say more, Jen?'

We all need to avoid talking over people. Let people finish their point, even if you disagree with them. However, there is a balance to be struck between giving people the floor and having them dominate the conversation.

You can deal with people who dominate meetings by saying something like:

- 'So the main point you are making is [summarise point], yes?'

- 'Could you summarise your main point, please?'

- 'We've heard from David and Fiona, what does everyone else think about X?'

In circumstances of severe stress (eg crisis meetings), women's voices are even more likely to be drowned out, despite being a time when a good manager should be seeking input from a range of people. Stephen remembers talking to a female support engineer who recalled a technical problem with a live system. She was on a conference call where the issue was being discussed, and knew the piece of technology that had failed better than the rest of the group, who were all male. She told them repeatedly what the problem was, but no-one would listen. In the end, she hung up, turned to her colleague and said, 'They'll call me back eventually when they realise I was right and need my help.'

Much of accidental gender bias is about poor communication. Meetings – which we all have too many of – are a key setting for poor communication, so ask for training on how to chair, provide training if you are in a position to offer it and rotate the chairs of meetings or for different agenda items so that everyone improves their skills in this vital area.

Language barriers

A common conversation we have with men when talking about inclusive behaviours is around language. Our conversations with women reveal that continual use of phrases such as those we've included below can exacerbate a woman's feeling of not belonging. This topic generates debate and it is fair to say that some of the examples we've given are dependent on context, but unless you are sure they won't be misconstrued it would be safer to avoid these phrases altogether.

Examples of non-inclusive language include:

- 'That was a blonde moment.'

- Phrases like 'stop nagging' play to a well-worn stereotype. There are plenty of alternatives that can be used if someone feels that they are getting unwanted advice or ideas.

- 'Come on, ladies', particularly when talking to a group of men, the implication being that women are not punctual or do not demonstrate urgency.

- 'She needs to man up', 'She took it like a man' or, 'She needs to grow a pair.' This implies that women need to act more like men to succeed or that men show more determination in the face of adversity than women.

- Referring to women as 'girls' (implying immaturity) or 'ladies' (in a context where you wouldn't say gentlemen).

And yes, we know that women use these phrases too. It doesn't make it right. Our recommendation is to use the words woman/women or female, when appropriate. When we made this point at a large conference, a CEO expressed outrage at the idea that he could no longer use the word 'ladies'. As we mentioned, context is important. There is no issue with using the phrase 'ladies and gentlemen' in the right setting, but if you wouldn't say 'gentlemen' then you shouldn't say 'ladies'.

We also suggest avoiding gender qualifiers – for example, 'female developer', 'female journalist', 'female doctor'. In almost all cases, the female qualifier is not needed and serves to diminish the woman's role.

Our overriding message here is that language must be thought about carefully. By picking up on it and making a habit of using different words, you can make a real difference. Again, how and when you do this depends on your status within a team, how well you know the people involved and your personal style. It is easier and more effective for the most senior people to do this in public, in the moment. Individuals who know and feel comfortable with their team members can do the same. However, many individuals acting as allies may feel it is safer to have these conversations after the meeting, one on one.

Beware of banter

It's important to look out for men trying a bit too hard to engage a female colleague's attention, or who are having inappropriate conversations or, worse still, staring or making comments when women walk past. Similarly, there could be times when a man is making excessive contact with a certain woman in the team or men are specifically 'checking out' a woman. In our experience, in a male-dominated environment these problems are mostly caused by men initiating unwelcome attention. However, men in junior positions have also reported senior women making them feel uncomfortable by flirting, or commenting on their looks or clothes, even in jest.

Difficult though it might be, these are the times for senior people to step in. Our advice is to check first with the recipient of the problematic comment, saying you would like to tackle this and seeking their permission to intervene with the perpetrator, their manager or even HR. This means dealing with the issue after the event. There will also be occasions when a senior manager, team leader or team member feels safe to intervene in the moment. One useful piece of learning from research is that other men in the team are more likely to actively support your intervention than you may think.[12]

Don't accept the dreaded phrase, 'It's just harmless banter.' Behaviours can be interpreted differently depending upon the context and the level of trust between people, but the most important thing is how these social interactions are perceived by those involved. If it is making anyone in your team feel uncomfortable, that behaviour has to stop.

Every company should have policies and procedures to deal with sexual harassment, bullying or worse. That said, a complainant does not always want to take what some see as the nuclear option of raising a grievance with HR or one's line manager. Several organisations offer a middle way. Trained advocates are available to listen and help you talk through an issue, however unsure you are about what's happening and how you feel about it. Advocates can also explain the courses of action available to you. An example of this is the Inclusion Advocate programme started in the law firm Clifford Chance.[13] We found that creating an allies network similarly provided an alternative path for people to raise concerns, as the senior allies were seen as a sympathetic ear and someone who could be approached for advice.

How to call something out

Now you are more aware of accidental sexism, we have some tips on how to call out sexist, including subtly sexist, behaviour. The examples here can be used by men or women who witness examples of accidental sexism or who experience it themselves. Remember that all genders can act in accidentally sexist ways and that it is helpful, psychologically safer and more comfortable for someone experiencing sexism to have an ally intervene on their behalf. It can be helpful to rehearse a few phrases that you can turn to – practise and, as you become more confident, make changes so that you can intervene in the way you feel most comfortable.

First, you need to choose whether to comment in the moment or after the event. You can ask for permission to follow up on an issue by saying something like, 'I'm going to think about it and come back and talk to you later.' You should use 'I' statements. Be specific. Talk about what you understood by the incident and how it made you feel. If you are bringing up an issue about something that was said, repeat the comment verbatim.

Think about your body language. Don't laugh at a remark you are uncomfortable with, or that one of your colleagues seems uncomfortable with. You can show disapproval by turning away and/or changing the subject, or hold up your hand in a 'stop' gesture and say something like:

- 'Can I just stop you there? What I understand by what you just said is...'

- 'I'm uncomfortable with that' or, 'I'm not sure how I feel about that...'

You can use humour, if that comes naturally to you. For example, a phrase that most people understand is: 'I'm yellow-carding you for that remark.' A questioning style can also be effective:

- 'How was that funny? I don't get it.'

- 'I'm not sure whether you realised...'

- 'I know you were trying to be funny when you said [repeat comment] but this is how it made me feel...'

- 'This is what I understood by [repeat comment/incident]. What did you intend?'

- 'I think we've come to different conclusions about this. Can you take me through your thinking?'

- 'What did you mean by [repeat comment]?'

- 'Are you aware that your comment could be interpreted as...?'

- 'Have you considered that women might experience that differently?'

- 'I wouldn't like you to inadvertently offend women by saying [repeat comment].'

- Ask if the language used in that situation/assessment would have been the same if they had been talking about a man. Or, more personally, their sister, or mother or female partner.

Being able to call things out does, of course, need leaders to make it safe to do so by setting an example and supporting others. This is necessary to help people call out someone higher up the hierarchy than them.

What to do and say when you are called out

If you are called out for accidentally sexist behaviour or language yourself, when responding, start from the understanding that this is difficult and emotionally tiring for the person who is raising an issue. It's your responsibility to take them seriously and find a solution. Below are some suggestions you can try out and tailor to what feels right for you.

Do say:

- 'I'm sorry. That was not my intention. It's clear I've got some work to do. I want to try to make this right. If you have the time, and want to, can you suggest what I should have said or done instead?'
- 'I'm listening. I appreciate you bringing this up.'
- 'I'm going to reflect on what you've said and come back to you soon.'
- 'I'm sorry. I intend to do better.'

Don't say:

- 'You must have misunderstood.'
- 'No, you must have imagined that.'
- 'Oh, it was just a joke.'
- 'I don't know why you are so upset.'
- 'You are being over-sensitive.'
- 'That's just me being me.'

Key takeaways

This chapter has focused on the everyday behaviours that many men don't notice but that have a big impact on women's access to equality of opportunity. The examples we've given are themed around the 5Cs: capability, constraints, connections, credit and communication.

When you notice these behaviours, male allies have a powerful and necessary role to play in intervening to move these obstacles out of the way. We've given advice about everyday ways men or women can intervene to tackle these issues, what kind of behaviour or language to call out, how to do so and, importantly, we finished this chapter with advice on what to do if you find yourself being called out for accidentally sexist behaviour. Practise these interventions so that, over time, they become comfortable and easy for you to do.

The next chapter gives our top tips for making your hiring practices more inclusive and for increasing the number of women in your team, department or company.

Chapter 5

Improving The Hiring Process

Hiring is tough at the best of times, but if you want to improve the gender balance of your company, you must think about how you can attract more female applicants. In this chapter, we focus on the steps that hiring managers (and their managers) can take to recruit talented people who also happen to be women – including women who are also members of other minority groups such as women of colour. It is worth noting that many of these ideas are also relevant to improving hiring outcomes with other traditionally under-represented groups.

Setting expectations

We often hear managers cite the low percentage of the graduate pipeline that is female, expecting the pool of female candidates for a particular specialty or senior role to be similar or lower, and lower still for female candidates of colour. The problem with low expectations is that they can be self-fulfilling. When you don't expect many candidates from under-represented groups to apply and expect to hire even fewer of them, you have no incentive to be more flexible in the way you find candidates or to scrutinise your recruitment processes for bias. There are also fewer women actively looking for a job because women tend to switch employers less often than men and the global pandemic has led to more women in management dropping out of employment or cutting back their hours.[1,2,3] In short, it is easy for people to continue to hire mostly white men and blame this on external factors. The implication is that in order to accrue the benefits of diverse hiring for your teams, one has to start with the *intention* to hire women, and women of colour. New approaches are needed.

The first thing we recommend is to make it clear to hiring managers that interviewing at least one female candidate is mandatory for every role and that they should not expect to make a hiring decision unless they have seen a diverse set of candidates. You should take steps to ensure applicants are diverse at a higher rate than the target population, so if you have a shortlist of, say, ten candidates for a particular role and you think there are about 20% women in that type of role, aim to include three or four women in your shortlist. The same is true for how you'd want to think about other under-represented groups.

Job descriptions designed for diversity

Job descriptions are important because, if you don't get them right, you could be putting off a whole range of candidates (not just women) from the get-go. There is a lot of research that suggests men and women have different perspectives and approaches when it comes to evaluating risk.[4] This is a fascinating area and there are competing views on whether gender-related differences in approach to risk are genetic or whether other factors (eg stress, social standing, privilege) are the more likely determinants of risk appetite.[5]

One recurring theme in this area is differing behaviours when it comes to applying for jobs. Research has shown that women only apply for open roles if they think they meet 100% of the criteria, whereas men apply if they think they meet 60% of the criteria.[6,7] Similarly, research from LinkedIn found that women apply for 20% fewer jobs than men, and are 16% less likely than men to apply for a job after viewing it.[8] Why is this? The research is not completely clear. There could be a link to the difference in risk appetite, or it could be that women lack confidence if either they have been out of the workplace for a while (eg for parental leave – which they are more likely to have taken than a man) or because they have experienced continual bias against them in their current role. Or perhaps they believe the hiring process is biased against them (which it is, in a lot of instances). Another possibility, highlighted in Robin Ely's and Irene Padavic's 'What's really holding women back?' is that women are more likely than men to have been conditioned since school to follow the rules.[9] It is most likely a combination of these factors, but the key point is to be aware of the difference.

In light of this, companies should take a long hard look at the job descriptions they use and think about how much they allow individual managers to tailor them. What skills and experience are truly essential and what can people be trained in or learn on the job? It may be worth making job descriptions more generic, with a focus on mindset and behaviours rather than specific skills. Ultimately, you are not hiring someone for a role but for your organisation. If you treat them well and they do a great job, then they will progress to a different role within the organisation and will learn different skills along the way.

If people are allowed to write job definitions for roles they want to hire for, they should be trained in how to do it. There are a number of software tools that can make job descriptions more gender neutral.[10] As well as gender pronouns, these highlight language that tends to appeal to men and alienate women.

How to find more external applicants

When using an agency or a dedicated internal recruitment team to market a role and attract applications, have an early conversation with the recruiter to let them know you expect to see CVs from underrepresented groups. Ask for feedback on whether the job specification is likely to attract these candidates and how to improve it if not.

Next, look at leveraging your own network. In particular, make sure you're well connected to networking groups representing diverse communities in your industry and make yourself visible to these groups through industry events or a social media presence via platforms like LinkedIn.

Find out if there are any hiring programmes in your organisation that might improve your chances of attracting candidates from diverse backgrounds. For example, at our firm, a number of successful candidates have come through our return to work programme, which targets people who have taken a career break and are looking to get back into the industry. Another approach is to look at who does a good job of hiring candidates from diverse backgrounds in your organisation and ask them for tips.

If hiring candidates in bulk, when you have around ten or more similar roles, try consultancies who use alternative hiring methods to attract a diverse range of candidates and will contract staff with a 'right to hire' option for the candidates after the contract has been completed. These companies typically focus less on grades and degrees and instead use aptitude tests to identify candidates and then provide training to bring them up to a level where they can perform the required role. Some also target returning mothers and veterans to tap into non-traditional hiring areas.

If, after this, you are still not attracting diverse candidates, another option is a targeted hiring drive. We have run a few events where we have recruiters reach out using their contacts and social media platforms to candidates from diverse backgrounds who have the types of skills we are looking for and invite them to a career event at our firm. We aim to have fifty to one hundred candidates attend and invite all internal teams with open roles to come. We try to pair employees up with potential candidates so that they can interview and even offer roles there and then. Our Male Allies team has been invited to these events to demonstrate that support for women in technology is taken seriously by the firm.

Internal candidates

For more senior roles, we'd suggest you look at whether there is someone in your existing team who can step up into the role. It should be noted that biases in hiring managers can result in diversity being accidentally overlooked in such a process, so this needs to be done carefully. The first bias that can affect the selection of female candidates for internal roles is benevolent sexism. Typically, a manager might make well-intentioned (though often incorrect) assumptions about what type of opportunities a person might be interested in. For example, assuming, without asking, that a mother wouldn't be interested in a role with regular travel or that a newlywed woman wouldn't be interested in relocating.

The second bias that can cause female candidates to be overlooked is the affinity bias, or homophily bias, we talked about in Chapter 1. At work, we often have closer relationships with people 'like us'. The impact this can have when filling roles with internal candidates is that these people come more readily to mind.

To address both of these biases, it is best to take a structured approach to looking for potential candidates for the role. For example, if the role is for a vice president (VP) in marketing, look at all your existing VPs and people who are on your promotion radar for VP and go through the list one by one to identify potential candidates for the role. When you have your list of potential candidates, talk to them about the opportunity without making assumptions about whether they would be interested. This will, at least, ensure that everyone is considered.

Another approach is recognising when women are less likely than men to apply for promotions and actively inviting them to do so. For example, law firms often have elected places on the board and have typically elected fewer women. One firm we talked to bucked this trend by soliciting the opinion of existing board members on who they thought were good candidates for board seats and would like to apply. Communicating this to those nominated encouraged more talented women to apply and, unsurprisingly, has led to more women being elected to the board.

Finally, a number of the points made previously about external candidates also apply to internal candidates. Leverage your internal network, particularly diverse networking groups, to publish and advertise roles and see if women from other parts of the business may be interested in applying. Look for teams with greater diversity than yours and that are likely to have people with skills that will transfer into the role in question. For example, in technology we considered highly skilled women in other parts of the business, such as operations, who might be interested in a technology role.

Screening CVs

As we saw in the coding story from Chapter 2, there can be bias against women if their gender is known (studies have found a similar bias against people with names that suggest a racial minority).[11,12] To avoid bias in the initial review you could adopt a 'blind CVs' practice where people's names and any gender pronouns are removed. The screening process, however, will often involve some form of contact where gender is clear. We recommend setting clear criteria for identifying which candidates should be being interviewed. Biases are more likely to have an impact if the criteria are not clear, as the decision is then more likely to be based on intuition or 'a feeling' than a specific set of criteria.

Automated software that evaluates and screens candidates should be used with care as it may rely on inherently biased data to make evaluations. A good example of this is a recruitment machine-learning engine built by a team at Amazon.[13,14,15] The engine was trained on the CVs of successful and unsuccessful candidates from the last ten years, with the aim of learning which candidates were likely to be hired and thus save time reviewing CVs and interviewing. What the team found was that the algorithm learned that male candidates were preferred, as most of the successful hires in the dataset used to train the model were men. Despite not having access to the candidates' gender, the algorithm automatically marked down CVs likely to be from women, such as candidates who had attended women-only colleges. The algorithm also increased the rank of CVs containing words more often used by men, such as 'executed' or 'captured'. After trying to fix the algorithm,

Amazon abandoned the system and the team was disbanded in 2017.

If, after the screening process, you are finding that few candidates from diverse backgrounds make it through, we recommend adding back in a few of the candidates who have been filtered out and taking them through to the next round. By watching how these candidates fare, you may be able to spot a bias in the screening process. Another benefit is that, even if they aren't suitable for the role you are screening for, they may prove suitable for other roles in the company.

The interview process

Once you have your list of candidates, it is time to consider how you approach interviews. Are you doing everything you can to remove bias from the process? Let's look at a famous example.

In 1952, the Boston Symphony Orchestra decided that they needed to recruit more women and so created a 'blind audition' process whereby the applicant would be asked to play a piece of music from behind a screen. The initial results were surprising, as they did not hire women at a greater rate. They realised that the gender of the applicant was likely still known because the audition panel could guess it from the noise the applicant's footsteps made as they walked onto the stage. Only when they asked candidates to remove their footwear, did they see an increase in the number of women being hired.

Multiple orchestras followed suit and a study found that blind auditions made a significant difference to female hiring rates in the sector.[16] Some of the statistics in this report have subsequently been challenged but the overall body of evidence supports that taking this particular positive action made a difference to the gender make-up of orchestras without compromising on the quality of the performance.

We are not necessarily advocating that companies conduct blind interviews but it is certainly worth considering whether a change in the process is required. If you don't see a percentage of successful female hires that is in proportion with the percentage of female applicants, there is likely something stopping women from making it through the interview process.

We have eight recommendations for reducing bias in the interview process:

1. Use standard skills tests where possible so all candidates are tested on their ability to solve a particular problem. The more the interview is standardised, the less likely it is that interview bias will creep into the process.

2. Have a diverse set of interviewers. This is valuable for a few reasons. First, having diversity here will help reduce the impact of any

unconscious biases in interviewers, or at least make sure the biases are diverse. Second, it will help sell the organisation to candidates from diverse backgrounds if they can see people like them already in the post and part of the interview process. Third, a range of interviewers will help to test the candidate on how they interact with a diverse set of people, to ensure they can work effectively with people not like themselves.

3. Make sure the interviewers have had interview training and know what not to ask. I (Stephen) am often surprised when I interview for a job, how many people ask about my family and hobbies. When this happens, I think how difficult it must be for some people to answer those types of question. I know the interviewer is typically making small talk but I do wonder why they would want to know. Nothing useful can come of asking personal questions in interviews and the risk is you hear something that influences your judgement of the candidate but that has no bearing on whether they could do the job. If you need to ask some warm-up questions to put the candidate at ease, stick to the weather or the journey to the interview.

4. Ask the same questions with all of the candidates, in the same order. Research has shown that women are more likely than men to be interrupted in interviews and are asked

more follow-up questions – by women as well as men – so be aware of this.[17] This happens because women are more commonly asked to prove their skills than men (ability bias), which gives female candidates less time to sell themselves. Asking the same questions and giving people the same amount of airtime (as far as possible) will reduce the impact of bias and help make fair comparison.

5. Think about the person's potential. There is research that shows men get hired more often on potential rather than actual experience.[18] We generally suggest to male hiring managers to think more about potential, especially when it comes to women, particularly if they could not easily demonstrate the incredibly long list of skills that may have been written on the job description.

6. Score answers, as they are given, on a scale of one to ten; this reduces the dependence on memory, which can hinder objective evaluation because we are more likely to remember the most recent answers, the most vivid, or those of candidates who use a story-telling approach in giving their responses.[19]

7. When discussing the candidates after the interviews, it is good practice to discuss candidates' responses question by question, rather than comparing one candidate with another overall. This also combats affinity and ability bias.[20]

8. If conducting panel or group interviews, consider making one of the panel a 'bias spotter' tasked with picking up on bad practice during the interview or in the post-interview debrief.

Selecting the successful candidate

Once all of interviews have been completed, the hiring manager will want to get feedback on the candidates before deciding who to offer the role to, a decision they will typically make with their manager. Should you find yourself in the position of making a hiring decision, there are a few additional things to bear in mind before making the final selection:

1. Are you comfortable with the hiring process?

2. Have enough suitably qualified candidates from under-represented groups been interviewed? If not, consider delaying the final decision and instructing the hiring team to look for more candidates before making a hiring decision.

3. When reviewing the interview feedback, consider the make-up of the current team and look for what is missing and what the potential candidates could add to the team. This could be language skills, a different background, or membership of an under-represented group – it is important that the benefit this diversity brings is factored into the hiring decision.

4. Ask questions about any candidate from a minority group who has been scored less well than others and yet is still recommended for hiring. The reasoning behind this is important. As we've already mentioned, we have come across examples of positive discrimination that would be unfair to anyone appointed under such circumstances.

Selling the role to female candidates

Assuming you find a woman you would like to offer the role to, how do you go about persuading her that this is the right organisation for her? Along with all your standard benefits, it is worth highlighting the organisation's commitment to inclusion. Make clear that not only are there multiple Employee Resource Groups, but that all employees are encouraged to embrace the organisation's values and facilitate the candidate's success with a positive attitude, flexibility and an outcome-focused mindset.

Research has shown that men and women value different things when selecting a role. A survey of over 1,000 men and women in the US showed that women favoured flexible work arrangements, work–life balance, shorter commutes and knowledge of how the company would develop their career. Men, by contrast, were more focused on financial success and so were more influenced by, for example, the financial performance of the company.[21]

How are you doing?

Improving the diversity of your hires is a slow and steady process and it will take time to assess the impact of any changes you make. It is too easy to recall a few recent diverse hires and think you are doing well without looking at the data. The measure you are looking to improve is overall diversity, so it is important you monitor this regularly as well as the diversity of your hires. Our experience is that it is also important to look at diversity at different levels of the organisation or department hierarchy. Often, hiring candidates from under-represented backgrounds becomes increasingly difficult the more senior the role.

Look also at the candidates with diverse backgrounds that you don't hire, either because they turn down your offer or because they drop out of the process at a late stage. Check why this happened. Find out who interviewed the candidate. It might be that guidance on having a diverse panel hasn't been followed or other best practices have been missed. If a candidate declined an offer because they didn't feel comfortable with the team or were treated badly in the interview process, you are unlikely to get this feedback via the hiring process. We suggest asking someone else to follow up with the candidate and verify the reason.

Stephen shares an example of this in our workshop, describing an occasion where a promising female candidate turned down a role in his group:

> 'I was told she did this because she wanted to work from home full-time. It didn't sound right to me that she would have expected this particular role to entail full-time work from home. Checking with the candidate, I found that she'd had a negative experience with the hiring manager. He was dismissive, didn't follow up, was late for the interview and generally left her with a bad impression. Even though we lost the candidate we were at least able to improve the interview process because of her feedback.'

Key takeaways

This chapter has provided our top tips for making your hiring practices more inclusive to increase the number of women in your team, department or organisation. These tips also apply to recruiting women or men who are members of other under-represented groups. We've looked at best practice for recruiting both internal and external candidates, at different stages of the process, including:

- Setting targets and expectations

- Writing more effective job descriptions

- How to find potential candidates from under-represented groups

- Avoiding bias from the first screening, through the interview process, to the role of the most senior managers in reviewing the hiring recommendations of the interview panel

- Selling the role to promising candidates

- Reviewing the outcomes

In the next chapter, we will look at what those who manage people can do to create a more inclusive culture, retain talent and manage career development.

Chapter 6

Retaining Talent And Managing Careers

This chapter is aimed at managers of people. They are on the front line when it comes to building the kind of inclusive environment that encourages retention and supports career development. We look at actions they can take to improve the way the whole team talks to and understands each other; how to address working hours and periods of leave; and other ways of facilitating career development, such as mentoring and sponsorship. Clearly, many of these actions also need to be supported by organisational processes and initiatives, so some of these ideas will prompt a discussion with the leadership team who are in a position to change these policies.

Better conversations

Probably the most common piece of advice we give to managers is to have more conversations. Many issues between managers and their team members arise from decisions made with good intent but influenced by biases, especially if a manager makes assumptions without talking to their employees. When managers get to know people better and discuss their issues more regularly, all sorts of inclusion issues can be quickly eradicated.

It is, therefore, helpful for organisations to define and communicate some expectations of all managers of people – and to check that these expectations are well understood. Such expectations could include, but not be limited to:

- A regular one-to-one meeting with all members of their team

- For those one to ones to include not only discussions about tasks and projects, but also personal development conversations about career advancement and learning

- Managers should try to understand the lived experience of their employees, within the boundaries of what employees are willing to share – no-one should be forced to divulge anything they are uncomfortable sharing

- Regular team meetings that include all team members

- Team meetings set at a time and place that enables all members to attend on a regular basis; if this means that meetings need to vary in place and time to ensure people with different work situations can attend, this should be done

- Everyone in the team should be given an opportunity to contribute in meetings; managers should ensure everyone's views are heard whenever possible and solicit peoples' views if they appear to need help to contribute

- For managers of managers, conduct regular meetings with staff more than one level below – ie those who are managed by a person reporting to you – either one to one or in groups

- For a departmental manager, a 'town hall' type event that allows the whole department to interact should be run on a regular basis (minimum of once a year, but preferably quarterly)

It's not only the regularity of conversations that matters. Improving the way we speak to and understand each other is vital. Feeling that you don't belong or have not been taken seriously can sometimes be down to a misunderstanding, a disparity between what managers think they have said and what members of their team have heard. Other times, what's happening is that feedback has not been given in a clear way, so it is interpreted as unfair or it is impossible to take action. We often hear examples of women being told they need to seem more confident or to have more gravitas. This is not necessarily problematic feedback. What causes problems is when this is not followed up by explaining how the woman in question could demonstrate confidence or gravitas and what that would look like in comparison to how she is currently coming across. Academic research tells us that the feedback given to women is often less direct and actionable than the feedback given to men.[1] The explanations given for this are concern about upsetting women, fear of coming across as a bully or not being able to articulate what a non-alpha male version of confidence and gravitas looks like.

Actions that managers can take to improve the feedback they are giving and getting range from small changes at an individual level, to profound changes in management style toward a coaching or facilitating style. Both ends of this spectrum can be supported by training. Actions you can take today include:

1. **Be more specific** when explaining what you are asking people to do or change.

2. **Listen better** by checking with people what they are hearing. This will help you avoid or correct misunderstandings. There are readily available tools to help with this, such as active listening courses on LinkedIn Learning.

3. **Ensure feedback is actionable** and the person has a clear idea of what behaviour needs to change, and how.

4. **Ask for feedback** – be proactive and check that people feel heard.

Career development

Evaluating performance

In light of research that shows men frequently get more credit than women for their work, it is worth reminding yourself of biases that affect managers' evaluations of the performance of their team members.[2] We discussed this earlier, in Chapter 1. Look at what your employee has written in their evaluation form or is saying about the work they have done and verify what they have achieved, and how they have achieved it, to ensure the process is fair and consistent. If your organisation does not have a formal feedback or peer assessment process, actively reach out to get views from others. For men, look out for the gendered language that another man might use that will instinctively appeal to you. Performance evaluation season is a good time for a refresher on your accidental biases.

Similarly, when it comes to objective setting, make sure that these are communicated with consistent language and expectations across all your employees.

New opportunities

We have come across several examples of women who are reluctant to switch roles or take up new opportunities. Gary has often shared a story about a woman who was doing an excellent job running software testing activities for a team he led in India:

> 'When my software engineering lead decided to move back to the US, I asked her to take over running the engineering team. She said no, because she felt she did not have direct experience of being an engineer herself. I felt that she had demonstrated her technical capability with the automation work she had done with the testing team and was convinced she was the right person for the role. It took me three months, but eventually I persuaded her and she has gone on to have an exceptional career as a software engineering lead.'

This experience of women being reluctant to move roles, even when they recognise that it would benefit their career, is one we have seen multiple times. We are not suggesting that this is a universal issue for women, but our advice to managers is to take time to understand any reticence on the part of those who you think have potential. Assuming you are having regular conversations about career development and new opportunities (as per our advice), you might need to work harder to support and encourage some people to take opportunities that will progress their careers.

Not all advice is good advice

Another area that managers need to actively address is career advice and role selection, to ensure women are retained in core or technical roles. From our experience in the IT industry we have found that, over time, women are encouraged to move into less technical roles such as project management, business analysis or team coaching roles that take them away from the core area for the organisation, which is software development, limiting future career progression.

Academic researchers Ely and Padavic completed an eighteen-month review of a global consulting firm into how its culture might be hampering women's progress. They showed that women who took advantage of work/family accommodations designed to help them, such as moving to an internally facing role or going part-time in practice, derailed their careers.[3] Women were also being advised by managers and mentors to change their style with clients from a relationship-focused one to a more aggressive masculine style. This caused women to step back from client-facing roles.

Speaking to leaders in the construction industry, they have told us they see similar trends in their industry, where female representation is higher in careers related to pre-build and interiors and much lower in operations. In both cases, women are moving into roles that do not tend to lead to promotion into the most senior positions in their organisations, unless a lot of work is done to make up the deficit in the skills that are needed for these senior roles.

Encouraging women into these less core roles is due to a conscious or unconscious bias that women don't belong in these technical roles. The consequences of these moves are typically not felt for a number of years, so often the manager who encourages that initial switch in career path will be unaware of the impact. Women are particularly vulnerable to this kind of biased advice after returning from maternity leave, when their managers might think that their technical skills will have atrophied and so be out of date.

Organisations must find a way to categorise roles and pay close attention if it seems women are switching to a less technical or less business-facing career track, to ensure that the motivations for and future implications of the change are discussed and agreed between manager and employee.

Mentoring

Many organisations initiate mentoring programmes, either firm-wide or targeted at under-represented groups in the organisation. We have much experience of these types of programmes at different firms, both from acting as a mentor and from allocating mentorship pairings. We have learned that mentoring can be a useful tool for supporting women, but to get the best out of mentors and mentoring programmes they need to be used selectively.

Broad brush mentoring programmes, where everyone is encouraged to have a mentor and the pairing is determined centrally by people who don't know either participant, tend to be hit and miss. Often, these relationships peter out after one or two meetings and create little lasting benefit. What we have found works best is for the manager to have a specific purpose in mind and find a mentor with experience in that particular area. Mentoring can be particularly helpful when someone has returned from a period of extended leave, is preparing for promotion, looking for new opportunities or developing expertise in a particular functional or technical area. Managers are often well placed to identify where the women in their organisations need more support and should know their employees well enough to pair them with someone whose experience and personality is a good fit.

There are benefits too for the mentors. Particularly for male managers, mentoring women can help them understand the experiences of women in the organisation. For example, Stephen found that helping a female mentee think through strategies to overcome the challenges she faced encouraged him to think about where there might be similar problems in his team and what he could do about them. In effect, the mentoring works both ways, as managers can gain insight into the lives of their junior colleagues, which can help make work a better place for everyone.

While mentoring can be useful in increasing people's sense of belonging and can help mentees navigate particular issues they face, research shows that mentoring has little effect on women's progression into senior leadership positions.[4,5] Career sponsorship is a much more effective tool for advancing to senior levels in an organisation.

Career sponsorship

While a mentor shares their experience and provides advice, a sponsor plays a more active role. A sponsor advocates for you, when you are not in the room. They can talk to others about your strengths and potential so that you are considered for development opportunities, promotion or the lateral moves that will help you acquire the skills you need for future senior roles. One opportunity tends to lead to another, and sponsors are there to help you adjust and thrive in a stretching role.

As a tool to address inclusion for women, formal sponsorship, with clear objectives and scrutiny, is needed to tackle the accidental biases that creep in with the 'tap on the shoulder' approach to opportunities that tend to occur naturally in organisations. Assigning a senior-level sponsor to act as an advocate for an individual woman, or a small group of women, has proven to be an effective way of clearing roadblocks to allow women to progress in the organisation and to develop more women into senior leadership roles. It's also a useful tool to use for promotions into mid-level roles to feed the future pipeline.[6]

Sponsorship works best as a formal business process, for three main reasons. First, identifying opportunities for lateral and hierarchical promotion requires a whole-organisation view. Second, making it a professional process takes away some of the reputational risk, or gossip, that individuals fear when focusing attention on individuals, particularly when those individuals are of a different gender. Third, sponsorship takes time, commitment and training to do well. Managers of people need to identify talent among their team to determine who would benefit; the sponsor then needs to take time to get to know the individual(s) they are sponsoring and perhaps help them recognise the potential that others see in them. A good sponsor will work with the person being sponsored to create a long-term roadmap of what stretch opportunities could look like, and update this over time. Ideally, this relationship should persist across multiple roles identified in the career roadmap.

Challenging long hours culture

There is increasing evidence that a long working hours culture is not conducive to positive work outcomes.[7,8] In fact, research shows that in companies or sectors that continue to insist on long hours, there is an additional impact on women that makes it less likely they will succeed in those organisations.[9,10]

Changing this culture is difficult. A lot of organisations see long hours as something to be proud of and, if challenged about changing it, will often push back. They will see it as a reason they are successful and will be concerned that shortening hours will have a negative impact on delivery, outcomes and profit.

As a manager, if you work within that kind of culture and believe it would be difficult to change it, there are still things you can do. First, set an example by making long hours the exception not the rule. Talk openly about your working practices and that you don't expect to always be working to a strict schedule. Sending emails out of hours is a clear signal that you expect everyone to be working twenty-four seven. One tip if you're answering emails out of hours is to save your replies in a draft and then send during normal working hours – although don't send them all at the same time so they result in a deluge for your team.

Likewise, if you are taking some time out (eg on holiday), do not stay in contact with your team and continue to send them emails, texts or other messages. First, this tells them that you don't trust them. Second, it tells your manager that you cannot delegate and have not developed your team to work effectively in your absence. Third, it means you are not getting downtime, which can lead to physical and mental health issues down the line if you are not careful.

Another way senior managers can challenge long hours culture is by making visible exits. While working for an investment bank in New York, Stephen managed a 100-plus global team working to tight regulatory deadlines in the aftermath of the Lehman crisis:

'I, like many others in my team, was working hard to upgrade the risk management capabilities of the firm and this inevitably led to us working long hours. Aside from my day job I was also a keen scuba diver and had started working on my instructor's certification at a scuba diving school. One Thursday, I decided to help with a scuba class to get some extra practice, so I needed to leave by 5pm that day. I had left the office early before but what was different this day was that I needed to take my scuba gear with me. It was pretty obvious I was leaving, as I could barely carry all of my gear and people had to open the doors for me.

'The next day, one of my senior team leads came over and said I'd made such a visible early exit that the team, and particularly a number of the men, felt I had implicitly given them permission to leave early for a reason that was important to them. I think it also helped that I had left for a hobby, because if a hobby was a good enough reason, then so must be a school sports day or play. This was the first time I understood that something as simple as leaving early, but loudly, could have that level of impact.'

Finally, our advice is to not sweat the small stuff. Allow your team to have plenty of latitude when times are normal. Assuming that you have ways of monitoring that your team is achieving what they need to, give them flexibility with time when you don't have urgent deadlines. There will undoubtedly be times when you need to ask more of your team, to stay late, come in early or work a weekend. Save the long, hard hours for when it's absolutely necessary.

CASE STUDY:
A GLIMPSE OF CONSTRUCTION'S FUTURE[11]

The construction industry is a male-dominated industry. One reason for this is the long hours culture, particularly as construction site locations can often mean long commutes for the team. Willmott Dixon is a construction company that has set an ambitious target of reaching gender parity by 2030. Having realised the long hours culture would be an impediment to achieving this, they have been trialling a new way of working, which they refer to as agile working, based on a number of key principles. These principles include: no-one is allowed on site for more than 45 hours a week, and must have two breaks a day; sitewide we encourage all meetings to be standing and last only a few minutes if possible; everyone takes their breaks together and staff are not allowed to discuss work; the last meeting of the day must finish by 3pm and the site must close by 5pm. Within these constraints, the teams could flexibly schedule their hours across the week.

On the first project where the new approach was trialled, many team members were unsure the plan would work and needed to be told to go home at the end of the day. However, the team persevered. Over time, the change took hold and the benefits started to become clear to the broader team. When their time on site was capped, people became more focused. The structured working week allowed people to leave early or arrive late as needed, to better support caring responsibilities or make the commute shorter. The project itself ran more smoothly, finishing seven weeks early and winning an award from the Considerate Constructors Scheme, while the project manager won a gold medal in his category at the prestigious Construction Manager of the Year awards. The new agile practices are now being rolled out to the company's other projects.

Managing extended leave of absence

This brings us on to dealing with extended leave of absence, the most common example of which is parental leave. Although things are slowly changing and more men are taking longer parental and even shared leave, maternity leave still has an impact on women's careers, which is why it is vital for managers to be thoughtful when dealing with it.[12]

First, managers need to make sure they are up to date on the firm's parental level practices. Our experience is that male managers rarely have a good understanding of the firm's policies and practices, particularly global managers, as policies often differ by country. As a result of this lack of understanding, we have had a number of reports from women who have been told things such as 'employees on maternity cover are not eligible for promotion', that they 'should be happy' with a much lower bonus or even that they are 'not eligible for bonuses or pay rises' – all of which were either incorrect or misinterpretations of the firm's policies.

When an employee is about to go on leave, it is good practice for their manager to establish an agreement on regular contact while they are away. Providing this is mutually agreed, it will help that person to still feel engaged with the team and up to speed on what is happening and how projects, client relationships and work activities are evolving. This arrangement must be flexible so that the employee on leave doesn't feel like they have to commit to a schedule of meetings. Our experience is that managers can be unnecessarily concerned about contacting people away on parenting leave, or may think they are doing the employee a favour by letting them have a complete break from work. Often, the person on leave wants to know what is happening and a lack of contact makes it much harder when they return to work.

Then, at the point the person is returning to work, the manager needs to have an honest conversation with their employee that should start with an open question like, 'What do you think this means for you?' How do they want to manage travel, client entertainment, their working hours and location? There are no right or wrong answers, but the manager must understand the perspective of their team member. For some people, it will become clear that work is going to take second priority, for a time, to managing their personal circumstances. Others will have childcare arrangements that enable them to pick up where they left off and may only need minor accommodations or flexibility. This needs to be a regular conversation rather than a one-off, as in most cases needs will change over time and working arrangements may require adjustment.

One final consideration is whether additional support is needed when the person returns to work. This is especially the case for those on extended leave, such as parenting leave in Europe, which can last a year or more. In some industries, like information technology, or jobs where the applications and tools required to do the job are rapidly evolving, consider offering some additional training or support to help the person get up to speed quickly and effectively.

Encouraging men to take parenting leave

More men taking parenting leave will do much to level the playing field and challenge the notion that caring is women's work. While many men want to take parenting leave, often they don't.[13] Making parenting leave the default and requiring people to opt out rather than opt in has been shown to improve take-up. Some companies are going further. Aviva, for example, now offer all their staff equal paid parental leave (EPL) of twenty-six weeks, irrespective of gender, sexual orientation or how they became a parent (birth, adoption or surrogacy).[14] They have supporting policies around backfilling roles during extended leave, linked to a broader talent management programme. Employees trust that no-one will be penalised for taking time out. As a result of these changes, new fathers at Aviva take an average of twenty-two weeks' parenting leave (compared to an average of two weeks before EPL) and 32% of these new fathers work flexibly upon returning.[15]

Other behaviours to watch out for

Another common issue is how managers talk to women about maternity leave. Male managers in particular can make assumptions, for example that women will not return to the same role. A seemingly innocent question like, 'What will you be doing when you come back from maternity leave?' betrays the assumption that it won't be the same as what they're doing now. Another example is assuming that the person won't return and acting as if they are leaving for good when they take maternity leave, saying things like, 'Thank you for all your hard work, best of luck for the future.'

Men can also make women feel uncomfortable in the run-up to or after maternity leave by making comments on their size, about breast-feeding, about hormones or forgetfulness, and other personal aspects of motherhood and childcare. It isn't easy to come back from an extended absence, particularly with the additional demands of a small child, so it is important managers are sensitive to how these comments might be perceived and look out for them so they can be addressed.

Key takeaways

The most senior leaders can set the tone and allow their employees the space and time to explore and implement more inclusive practices, yet it is middle managers who are in the engine room accelerating and embedding cultural change. In this chapter, we have outlined the key things those middle managers can do to make a difference. We have suggested building inclusive workplaces by improving communication and feedback, giving teams more control over how many hours they work and where, and facilitating career development. To deliver these changes, middle managers need time to learn and engage others. They also need support from policies and processes set by HR, finance and D&I leadership.

In the next chapter, we turn to promotion and compensation. Changing practices in these areas requires the most senior managers and HR leadership to take steps to support managers and individuals across the whole organisation.

Chapter 7

Promotion And Compensation Processes

In this chapter, we discuss the promotion and compensation processes adopted in organisations. These processes are critical to defining success in organisations, and so can help or hinder the progress of women, including women of colour. We will provide some recommendations for the organisational leaders who define and implement these processes, to help ensure they are fair. We will also discuss how to measure whether your strategies to build a diverse workplace are effective.

Promotion process

A problem revisited

As we reported in Chapter 1, many organisations have large numbers of women in entry-level roles, but they are not being promoted to senior roles at a rate that is in proportion to their numbers in mid-level roles and there are still large gender imbalances in higher-ranking positions.

Why aren't women being promoted? And what can be done to address this? Again, the biases and behaviours that we have covered in prior chapters come into play and affect promotion chances. This chapter covers how we see these processes working now and how the process can be made fairer.

A number of elements of the promotion process need to be considered:

- The selection and nomination process

- The promotion criteria

- The promotion evaluation

Promotion selection process

There are two main ways in which candidates are nominated for promotion in companies. The first is self-selection, where people put themselves forward, through either a formal or informal process. The second is where they are selected by their manager. It has been argued in several studies that women are more risk averse than men. We detail some of the research for this in the prior chapter. Hence it follows that women would be less likely than men to put themselves forward for promotion.[1] In our experience, this has been the case. We have seen many women successfully promoted who didn't think they were ready but were put forward by managers, mentors or sponsors. By contrast, we have seen relatively few examples of this happening with men. We recently came across an organisation that had an informal policy of a person needing to be seen to be 'pushing for promotion' before they would be considered eligible. Unsurprisingly the organisation found that men were far more likely to do this than women.

It is often the manager who puts candidates forward for promotion, and we know from research such as McKinsey and Company's Women in the Workplace study,[2] that managers are more likely to be male. Unfortunately, it is easy for these managers' decisions to be affected by in-group bias, or affinity bias, which will cause them to unintentionally favour male candidates and so reduces the number of women put forward for promotion.[3]

Another reason too few women are put forward is lack of knowledge of the process and policy around maternity leave. We have seen and heard of a number of cases of managers applying maternity policy incorrectly and excluding women from promotion. Organisations' policies and practices often make it clear that people should not be disadvantaged in their roles or promotion opportunities as a result of parental leave, yet promotion policies often include requirements that contradict this principle, such as 'must have spent one year in the role' or 'must have twelve months of consistent performance' at a certain level. Managers can interpret maternity leave as preventing the employee from meeting the criteria if they haven't worked this period of time unbroken, meaning they miss out on promotion for a year, or possibly multiple years if they have multiple children.

We have seen many organisations try to address the problem of too few women being put forward for promotion with leadership training sessions. The aim being to increase women's confidence and encourage them to put themselves forward for promotion. In our experience, this does help but doesn't address the root cause.

Our recommendations to improve the promotion selection process are:

- Have an objective set of selection criteria for promotion to account for potential manager biases. Criteria such as time in role and performance ranking are a good starting point to identify all potential candidates. This should help minimise the risk of the manager using more subjective criteria for picking people. If there are strong candidates who aren't being put forward, particularly those in under-represented groups, this process should identify these people and provoke a discussion about what is needed for them to take the next step.

- Provide managers with clear guidance on how flexible working and extended leave apply to the policies around promotion.

- If too few women are putting themselves forward, speak to them to find out why. The increased hours expected at the next level? Lack of role models? Leadership training can help here; however, it is important that organisations identify the root cause so that they understand the problem they need to address.

Promotion criteria

Most companies' promotion criteria are created by senior managers. Most senior managers are men, so the promotion criteria are likely to be framed according to the prejudices and biases of men. We're not suggesting this is intentional, nor that these biases are obvious. However, just as we've seen language in job specifications that appeals to one gender more than another, the same is true of promotion criteria. Our recommendation is to ensure that, when promotion criteria are being defined or updated, the panel is balanced and includes members of under-represented groups with practitioner roles. For example, you don't want the managers on the panel to be mostly white men with the under-represented groups coming from HR or other corporate functions.

Another consideration is to ensure the criteria reflect dedication to and leadership in improving diversity. While most companies talk about the importance of improving diversity, extracurricular activities, particularly those that focus on improving diversity, tend to carry little weight in the promotion criteria. There is often space on the bottom of the promotion recommendation form to fill in extra things the candidate does but this is rarely a key criteria. This is a problem because it means that the promotion guidelines are not aligned with the organisation's goals of improving diversity, which is sending a mixed message about the importance of these goals. This lack of clarity also impacts the promotion chances of under-represented groups more than the male majority given that, in our experience, under-represented groups tend to volunteer more in this area.

Promotion evaluation

Once candidates reach the promotion panel, you would hope that bias would be largely absent. Most organisations view selecting candidates for promotion as an important process and so put their brightest and best people forward for promotion panels. In our experience, these panels are well run and intended to be unbiased; however, they are rarely gender balanced and so unintentional biases can be a factor determining promotion.

There are various types of subtly biased behaviour to look out for. First, you might notice more scrutiny of female candidates and the discussion tends to run longer than for male candidates, suggesting that the panel is looking harder for a reason to say no. Second, the bar may not be set at a consistent level. People on the panel may stipulate that a female candidate needs to have particular experience to meet the standard, despite men having been promoted without meeting that criteria. Third, you may notice different assumptions are made about the contribution made by a woman compared to a man in a similar role, which can lead to the same contribution being weighted differently. For example, a key project delivered by a man is assumed to be down to his management, whereas for a woman questions are asked about whether it was she or the team who drove the delivery. This bias is supported by a research study that found when women published academic papers jointly with men they received less credit than their male collaborators.[4]

It is hard to address these issues in the promotion panel because of the seniority of the participants. One thing we have seen work is to task at least one person on the panel with specifically looking for gender bias or fairness in the review process. For example, this person checks whether a question would have been asked if the candidate was a man, looks at the time spent on and scrutiny given to each candidate to ensure it is consistent, and asks questions about peers in similar roles. Some companies use a red chair for this person as a visual symbol of their role.[5]

Summary of practical tips for an unbiased promotion process

In summary, here are our tips for making the promotion process as fair as possible:

- Make the promotion selection process more data-based, such as by automatically nominating candidates based on a set of objective criteria.

- Provide regular training for managers so that policies are clear regarding promotion of employees who have taken an extended leave of absence.

- Have a gender-balanced panel decide promotion criteria.

- Collect data and metrics on nominated candidates to look for progress or problems (though recognise that such data is only useful for large populations).

- Make the promotion panel (deciding promotion criteria/promotion hiring) as gender balanced as possible.

- Nominate someone in the promotion panel to look for gender bias to make sure the promotion process is fair to men and women.

Compensation

Another factor working against D&I efforts is the compensation system. We were once told by a senior manager at an investment bank, 'This year, I would argue not a single dollar of compensation was awarded on the basis of how well managers perform on improving diversity.'

Most private sector companies have a skills-based or performance-based component to how they compensate workers. Usually, there is a process at the end of the year to indicate the relative performance of individuals in the organisation and to determine pay increases and any other forms of compensation, such as bonuses or shares. Often, this approach to compensation is described as being merit-based or a 'pay for performance' system. It allows managers to reward the behaviours and delivery that they and the organisation value. However, a couple of questions trouble us:

- Why don't firms compensate people for improving diversity?

- Is this pay fair, or do gender biases impact pay for women?

Considering the first of these questions, you need to look at how the reward processes work at large companies. Typically, merit-based pay is determined mainly by the key function of the job. For example, salespeople are paid by whether they have met or exceeded sales targets. In technology roles, people are often compensated based on their contribution to key projects. Generally speaking, roles are paid based on their contribution to the firm's revenue or profit.

Sometimes, companies also allocate a small amount of compensation to reward corporate tasks that benefit the larger organisation, such as corporate leadership. However, few companies compensate for diversity. Few companies set targets for diversity and, if they do, these tend to be confined to corporate level rather than teams or departments. Having spoken to many people in HR and legal, the main reason for this is a concern that it will be interpreted as the firm having quotas for hiring women and lead to positive discrimination. As a result of not having targets for diversity, we have rarely seen any specific compensation allocated to improving diversity based on objective measures. Improving diversity is not compensated for directly.

Given the evidence that improving diversity improves the performance of an organisation, why doesn't paying for performance encourage managers to improve diversity? The first reason concerns the time horizon for compensation. Most compensation reviews are performed yearly, based on the previous twelve months' performance. Improving diversity in an organisation or department is a marathon rather than a sprint. For example, in a group that is replacing 10% of the workforce yearly and has 25% women in the organisation, if they are able to increase the proportion of hired women from 25% to 40% (which would be an impressive improvement) this will increase the diversity of the group by just 1.36% a year, assuming that the attrition of women and men is equal. It follows that individual managers will not be able to demonstrate significant improvement in the diversity of their teams in a year.

The second reason a person's contribution to improving diversity is not linked to their compensation is that the benefit gained from diversity initiatives is not typically concentrated in an individual's area of responsibility. We have highlighted that diversity can be improved by reviewing policies, creating networks of like-minded individuals, improving inclusion in an organisation, creating better promotion pipelines, improving the hiring process and many other areas. All of these actions create diffuse benefits at the organisational level. Unfortunately, this also means that the time most employees spend on diversity initiatives will not be considered in an assessment of their performance. If they are being judged on a set of narrow criteria related to their individual role, an individual focused only on their day job and not working towards greater diversity will score better against these criteria than one who has spread their efforts to encompass areas they are not being evaluated on. The consequence is that most companies are unintentionally paying people less who are focusing on organisational-level activities, and particularly improving diversity.

Note that this point applies to people whose day job is in a business function and for whom improving diversity is or should be one of many goals. A minority of people in organisations have specific roles focused on improving diversity and inclusion and these people are compensated based on the impact they make in this area. Improving diversity is, however, an organisational goal that will require the engagement of the majority of the organisation to make a material improvement. This is why an incentive to improve diversity needs to be embedded in the compensation process.

A broader approach

Some companies do have a review and compensation process that takes diversity into account. We spoke to one technology company about the innovative ideas adopted in their internal processes for promotion and compensation, which others can learn from.

They carried out a survey, asking what qualities the organisation valued and what qualities were expected from the leadership team and managers at the company. The results highlighted what employees expected from the firm and what was important to them in terms of the culture and environment: fairness in promotion processes, respect for employees, having a diverse leadership team and a diverse company.

Most companies' employees would likely highlight similar things. But this company baked these qualities into their compensation and review processes. This company adopted a 360-degree review process where a manager was rated by their employees, peers and line manager against these criteria and these ratings were translated into an NPS (Net Promoter Score). They then went a step further and made these NPS scores visible to the organisation and an important input for the compensation process. Two-thirds of compensation was based on how the manager had performed in their functional role and one-third on their relative NPS score. The company has found this to be an effective way of aligning the compensation process with the values of the firm. Notably, the firm also has a diverse leadership team and a substantive and large allies group of male managers. It is clear that diversity and inclusion is important to their leadership. One of the men who leads their inclusion workshops is also a senior sales manager in Europe. He said the time he spends creating a more inclusive workplace is just as important as meeting his sales targets.

Thinking about fair pay

Determining whether pay is fair is another important much-debated area. Based on our experience, we have some advice.

A key question is how you assess whether pay is fair. One common measure is to assess the gender pay gap of the firm. Companies typically report an adjusted gender pay gap, where they compare men and women in similar roles and adjust for location, performance, grades and other factors. Often, these measures show that pay is equal for men and women within 1–2%. In the UK, firms are also required to provide an unadjusted gender pay gap, where the average pay for women and men is compared. For managers and professionals across the UK, the pay gap is over 20%.[6] In certain industries, like investment banking, the gap is even larger, with some banks reporting pay gaps of over 40%.[7]

Both of these measures have flaws. The adjusted pay gap allows companies too much flexibility in how the comparison is made to be truly useful. For example, it relies on measures that can be subject to organisational bias, such as performance ranking and grade. This argument is currently being made by a class action of women at Microsoft.[8] The unadjusted pay gap is a true gap; however, what it highlights is the lack of women in senior and higher paid roles, so also isn't a good measure of whether men and women are paid equally for the same job.

What we have learned from our time in industry is that objective criteria for assessing pay increases like grade, performance, role and experience are useful tools for reducing some of the bias in setting pay and generally making the process of compensation fairer and less reliant on individual managers making decisions person by person. Assessments should separate absolute pay amount from percentage increase. This is necessary because we have often seen women (and some men) who are materially underpaid. A pay process based on percentage increases doesn't always raise these people up to market value, so it can take many years to fix pay inequities. This type of pay deficit is commonly due to the person being hired at too low an initial salary, or to pay/bonuses being cut due to working only a partial year (eg due to taking leave) and then not fully reinstated the next year.

Over the next few years, we expect to see increased use of data analysis to look for pay inequity. Already, factor analysis can tell you to what extent pay varies by factors you'd want to be independent of pay, such as gender or race. As machine-learning models become more widespread and better understood, we expect these will also be used to assess pay equity.

Summary of practical tips for compensation

Our tips for ensuring the compensation process reflects the organisation's goal of improving diversity are as follows:

- Review compensation criteria and assess how they reflect broader organisational goals.

- Assess how compensation criteria are being applied on the ground. If you are disadvantaging people who work on diversity, change the criteria.

- Create an NPS score for managers – even if it is only used for the top levels of the hierarchy, from the board down.

- Ensure there is a separate process to fix pay inequities that can't be addressed through the BAU (business as usual) compensation process.

What gets measured, gets done

It is important to collect metrics on the representation of minority groups at all levels of the hierarchy and share this information with leaders and managers so that they understand the current representation of minority groups and can monitor the impact of their diversity and inclusion efforts. Many companies are hesitant to share these metrics with anyone but the C-suite, which means too many managers lack information on representation in their groups or departments.

These metrics can highlight where specific groups are under-represented to allow actions to be more targeted. For example, the percentage of women in a team might look to be OK or improving, but when you break it down into the different grades in the organisation you might see that the percentage of women at senior levels is low. This could indicate that women aren't being promoted from the prior grade in the expected numbers, or that women are leaving from that grade in disproportionate numbers.

These metrics are also useful in talent reviews, to help the broader management team get to know the up-and-coming women in the organisation. The management team can then act to provide members of minority groups with opportunities, particularly if individuals are ready to move to a higher role or their current role isn't working out for them.

Sometimes, metrics are not needed and the lack of diversity in a team is self-evident. We have an example of this, where we saw an opportunity to change things that worked well. At one of our campus locations, a series of senior-level changes led to a leadership team severely lacking in diversity. To address this, the team (which Gary was a member of) invited people from each of our ERGs to join – not to represent their groups, but to contribute as leaders of the organisation and help set the programmes and policies for that location.

There were many benefits in this approach. First, it was a public commitment by our leadership team to making a change that would better reflect the diversity of the organisation. Second, it created an opportunity for emerging leaders to be involved in senior leadership activities. Lastly, it meant that the decisions being made were reflective of broader perspectives and experiences across the whole of the organisation.

Key takeaways

In previous chapters, we have looked at what individuals, teams and managers can do to hire, retain, and develop more women in organisations. The critical takeaway from this chapter is the steps that senior leaders must take to enable long-term change to stick.

First, the promotion process must be fair – and believed to be fair throughout the organisation. Employees in many companies we have spoken to frequently cite this as a problem. We recommend an end-to-end review of the process and transparent, clear communication to all employees about the approach and any changes made.

Second, changes to compensation processes that demonstrate that inclusive values are upheld and rewarded by the organisation will accelerate inclusive practices across the whole workforce, bringing about a sea change in the culture.

Chapter 8

The Way Forward: A Manifesto For Change

Activities or programmes designed to improve career outcomes for people of under-represented groups have increased exponentially in recent years. Most of us involved in diversity and inclusion initiatives genuinely believe things are improving for women at work. But, wow, it is taking forever. Why is that?

Our experience and research suggests it is a combination of factors, including lack of women taking STEM subjects in higher education, women continuing to do a disproportionate share of unpaid work at home, bias in organisations impacting hiring and promotion decisions and, lastly, lack of focused investment in diversity.

In this final chapter, we will explain where the focus for organisations needs to be over the coming decade. A more inclusive culture will be fundamental to making the organisations of the future successful. Spending on diversity and inclusion can no longer be seen as an optional, discretionary spend, but just as crucial to organisational strategy as finance, risk or sales and marketing.

Organisations have known for a long while now that employee engagement and motivation is the key to long-term success, but still they can be hesitant to invest at the levels required to get the most out of their employees. This needs to change, so here is what we recommend.

A values-led approach

Improving inclusion and diversity is hard and takes sustained effort. It is important to engage the whole organisation to make these improvements, so finding a way to do this is a vital part of the strategy.

It needs to start with a clear articulation of the purpose of the organisation and its values. It may be worth re-establishing these and giving employees a voice in identifying which values are important to them. If everyone has contributed these values, alignment with and belief in them are strengthened.

Once these values are set, all people- and community-related programmes should be aligned to them. Any programmes associated with the following topics could form part of an overall values-led approach:

- Diversity and inclusion

- ERGs (covering all under-represented groups, as well as working families, neuro-diversity, etc)

- Health and wellness (physical, mental, financial)

- Philanthropy

- Volunteering and community support

- Sustainability

- Employee engagement (social, celebration, appreciation)

Many employees in larger organisations are bombarded with disconnected communication about all of the good things that their employer is doing. They do not have the time to engage with all of them. Bringing all of this together, and saying to an employee, 'You are part of this' gives clarity. In other words, '*You* have chosen our values, now choose where you want to get engaged – it can be around inclusion, around volunteering, around sustainability or even all of them. But our shared values matter and this is how you can help.' A clear message makes it far easier for employees to engage.

Employee resource groups

The values-led approach does have implications for Employee Resource Groups (ERGs). At one level, these are essential for an organisation. It is important that people with shared backgrounds and experiences can gather to discuss those experiences and support each other in navigating the workplace. People like to feel that there are other people like them in the organisation. These forums are a valuable way to highlight a broader group of role models across the organisation, help promote the company to under-represented groups and give them an input on changes to policies and procedures.

A problem for many organisations is that messages around their commitment to diversity and inclusion can end up being dispersed across many small groups. The groups can naturally isolate and separate from the majority, so focus is needed to help the majority understand the experiences of these groups. This also means that issues important to these groups' sense of belonging and thus their performance are simply not being heard by a large percentage of the company's workforce.

Hence, these groups need to be aligned to the overarching values-led approach explained above. It is critical that investment and governance takes these groups into account.

Proper investment

For diversity and inclusion efforts to make a difference, proper investment is required. This is where many companies go wrong. Unfortunately, there are no cheap short-cuts here. A company needs to fully understand exactly what investment they need to make in their D&I strategies to be successful. Not just in terms of money, but time. It requires more time spent on education, especially for senior executives (who are already time poor). This investment is worth it: study after study has shown that diversity and inclusion, and the increased employee engagement it drives, improves the bottom line considerably.[1]

Bringing together all initiatives under an aligned values-led programme avoids dilution of effort, provides focus and brings efficiency. Diversity and inclusion needs to be treated like any other strategic programme for the firm, not as something sitting at the side of the desk, with its success dependent upon the level of discretionary effort made by a few well-meaning employees.

This values-led programme will need all of the governance, control, reviews and regular assessment as every other major programme of work. It will need constant re-investment, as change is driven by technology, economic realities and socio-political changes. Whenever belts are tightened, this strategic imperative needs to be well protected: a motivated and engaged workforce must remain the number one priority for a successful organisation.

The employee experience

Continuous focus on the employee will be key to organisations' success. Wherever possible, employees' interactions with the workplace should be positive. If employee happiness is critical to commercial success, then so too is making it easy for employees to do their job. Measuring employee happiness, inclusion and engagement is as important a metric as profit and loss and shareholder returns.

Focus on collaboration and continuous learning

One of the most important lessons from the Covid-19 pandemic was that no-one was quite ready for it. Some firms had pandemic plans, but they were often different to what was actually implemented. For example, many firms did not have standard video conferencing technology immediately available and had not thought about that in their pandemic plans, leading to hastily rolled out usage of Zoom, Teams and similar tools, with many employees struggling to get familiar with the new technology.

Having so many people working remotely made traditional top-down command and control systems much harder to manage. This meant that a lot of decision-making had to move to the teams themselves. In turn, this led to teams learning new skills. This is a positive development. Successful companies in the new world of work, which is changing so rapidly, will need to delegate decision-making to where it can be implemented quickly, particularly in a crisis situation.

Most important when in a crisis is how quickly people and teams can learn. They will need to evolve and change approaches. To do this successfully, they must be used to practising learning together. They must be used to collaborating remotely and effectively using a variety of different communication methods. People need to have an open mind and be curious about the world and the people around them.

This brings us back to diversity and inclusion. We know that diversity enables a depth of thought that can lead to better perspectives on where we are now and what possible futures might look like. An inclusive approach helps bring together those diverse views and creates an environment in which people can share them. A curious mindset and a willingness to be open and be part of difficult conversations is key to helping people learn.

When the world was turned upside down by Covid-19, it became clear just how important and valuable diversity was. Organisations were suddenly faced with a new set of challenges and needed to innovate quickly. Many studies have found that diversity increases innovation, so it is expected that more diverse companies will have fared better in the pandemic – though it will take some time before studies are able to confirm this.[2]

This ability to continuously learn is what will set teams (and organisations) apart in an increasingly complex world where no individual has all the answers and new ideas need to be created by the collective mind. In the words of Satya Nadella, Microsoft CEO, 'It's time to move from being know-it-alls to learn-it-alls.'[3]

The skills of the future

Human beings are incredible organisms. Although there is widespread concern about artificial intelligence and other emerging technologies removing large numbers of jobs, a historical perspective suggests that humans will adapt and learn the new skills that are required to continue to find reward and meaning in their working lives.

What types of skills are we talking about? This is not an exhaustive list, but here are a few ideas:

- Communication
- Creativity

- Technology skills (coding, scripting, etc)
- Data analysis
- Innovation
- Emotional intelligence
- Integrity
- Agility
- Adaptability
- Curiosity
- Empathy
- Resilience
- Dedication to learning and practice
- Cognitive diversity
- Inclusiveness
- Humility

Some of these are not skills, but behaviours. These behaviours, though, will increasingly come to be seen as skills that companies look for. In fact, some companies are already hiring based on values and behaviours over skill-sets.

In our experience, people who embrace diversity and inclusion in the workplace are far more likely to develop the skills on this list. This is because they start getting used to difficult conversations and realise that they need to know more about the lived experience of others. This requires greater humility, more curiosity and will lead to developing new ideas.

Companies should look at deploying coaches who can help teams to learn new skills or, more importantly, to learn how to embed a culture of continuous learning. A coach who can enable teams to question themselves, explore how to solve problems and create new innovative ways of working could be key, especially when teams can easily be overwhelmed with their day-to-day workload.

When it comes to inclusion, coaches can help teams practise what to do when someone says or does something that makes others uncomfortable, what to do if they are called out, as well as how to avoid gender-based language traps. They can coach teams through the inclusive practices we explored earlier in regard to performance review and promotion processes. Coaching can also help teams learn when they make mistakes (as we all do) rather than having unguided managers taking issues down the HR route.

Key takeaways

There are a number of levers that organisations can pull to affect culture change. To become a more inclusive workplace, all of them need to be considered, prioritised, implemented, reflected upon and re-implemented. Not all of these ideas will be relevant for every organisation, but in all cases, without gaining the support and commitment of everyone in the company, change will take a long time. All organisations should take a long hard look at their working practices and policies and adjust them to develop and build inclusive teams and incentivise managers to implement changes.

Hence, our final takeaways are less instructive and practical. They are about reflection; they are about organisations taking accountability; they are about considering how to make inclusion a strategic imperative. And to invest in it as you would all other similar business critical activities; to make the choice that this is not optional, but part of your reason as an organisation for existing. It is not only the right thing to do, but the right strategic decision. We are convinced that you will not regret it.

We hope you have enjoyed reading this book. We also hope that you have learned a few useful things. The most important thing we hope you'll take away from reading this book is a desire to take action, no matter how small. Wherever you are in terms of seniority, there is much that is in your power to do to make your workplace more inclusive. If you are a manager of people, there are many ideas here that you can introduce with your teams. If you consider yourself a leader, please implement some of these changes within your organisation.

If you have thoughts and ideas that you would like to share about any of the subjects covered in this book, we would love to hear from you. As we said at the start, we are still learning too. We would like to say a big thank you to all the people who helped us with our journeys. We appreciate the army of sympathetic voices, great listeners, people telling us when we made mistakes and genuinely passionate supporters who told us to keep going. For those who took the time to educate us, with great patience and humility, we are forever in your debt.

Finally, we hope that all of you, as individuals, have moved beyond knowing and understanding and started *feeling* how important this subject is, and that you want to get involved and be part of this change. If you are a man who has never been to a diversity event, now is the time to go. If you are a woman who has felt like nothing would ever change, now is the time to believe it can. For everyone, now is the time to start working and living differently. If you would like our help, we would be more than willing to talk to you.

You will all have heard the saying, 'accidents happen'. We are the accidental sexists who have learned the hard way. If this book makes those accidents a little less likely and, better still, averts a few of their awful outcomes then, in a small way, we will have achieved something.

We want to put all we have learned to good use. The authors, along with several like-minded colleagues, have started a consultancy called 'Men for Inclusion'. We offer advice about setting up male ally programmes, diversity dialogues that help you spot accidental sexism, and workshops on how to call out issues and change behaviours and cultures. You will find us at **www.theaccidentalsexist.com**

Useful Resources

Engaging male allies

Criado-Perez, C, *Invisible Women*, Vintage Publishing, 2019

Krivkovich, A et al, 'Women in the workplace 2020', McKinsey and Company, 2020, www.mckinsey.com/featured-insights/diversity-and-inclusion/women-in-the-workplace

Men as change agents

Armstrong, J and Ghaboos, J, 'Women collaborating with men: Everyday workplace inclusion', Murray

Edwards College, 2019, www.murrayedwards. cam.ac.uk/sites/default/files/files/Everyday%20 Workplace%20Inclusion_FINAL.pdf

Flood, M and Russell, G, 'Men make a difference: How to engage men on gender equality', Diversity Council Australia, 2017, www.dca.org.au/research/project/ engaging-men-gender-equality?

Prime, J and Moss-Racusin, CA, 'Report: Engaging men in gender initiatives', Catalyst, 2009, www. catalyst.org/research/engaging-men-in-gender-initiatives-what-change-agents-need-to-know

Resources for use in male allies workshops

Kimmel, M, 'Why gender equality is good for everyone – men included', TED Talk, 2015, www.ted.com/ talks/michael_kimmel_why_gender_equality_is_ good_for_everyone_men_included?language=en

Tinsley, CH and Ely, RJ, 'What most people get wrong about men and women', *Harvard Business Review*, 2018, https://hbr.org/2018/05/what-most-people-get-wrong-about-men-and-women

How to make changes

Recruitment and promotion processes

Bohnet, I, *What Works: Gender equality by design*, Harvard University Press, 2016

Individual behaviour changes

Anderson, RH, *We: Men, women, and the decisive formula for winning at work*, John Wiley and Sons, 2018

Catlin, K, *Better Allies*, Better Allies Press, 2019

References

Introduction

1. H Lee and MT Hicken, 'Death by a thousand cuts: The health implications of black respectability politics', *Souls*, 18/2–4, 2016, 421–445, https://doi.org/10.1080/10999949.2016.1230828
2. V Hunt, D Layton and S Prince, 'Why diversity matters', McKinsey and Company, 2015, www.mckinsey.com/business-functions/organization/our-insights/why-diversity-matters
3. A Franke, *Create a Gender Balanced Workplace*, Penguin Random House, 2019
4. RH Anderson, *We: Men, women and the decisive formula for winning at work*, John Wiley and Sons, 2018

5. S Vinnicombe, et al, 'The female FTSE board report 2020', Cranfield University, 2020, www. cranfield.ac.uk/som/research-centres/gender-leadership-and-inclusion-centre/female-ftse-board-report

6. A Krivkovich et al, 'Women in the workplace 2020', McKinsey and Company, 2020, www. mckinsey.com/featured-insights/diversity-and-inclusion/women-in-the-workplace

7. S Vinnicombe, et al, 'The female FTSE board report 2020', Cranfield University, 2020, www. cranfield.ac.uk/som/research-centres/gender-leadership-and-inclusion-centre/female-ftse-board-report

8. A Krivkovich et al, 'Women in the workplace 2020', McKinsey and Company, 2020, www. mckinsey.com/featured-insights/diversity-and-inclusion/women-in-the-workplace

9. J Armstrong, 'Collaborating with men: Changing workplace culture to be more inclusive for women', Murray Edwards College, 2017, www. murrayedwards.cam.ac.uk/sites/default/files/Collaborating%20with%20Men%20-%20FINAL%20Report.pdf

10. M Flood, G Russell and Diversity Council Australia, 'Engaging men on gender equality', Diversity Council Australia, 2017, www.dca.org. au/research/project/engaging-men-gender-equality?

11. D Rock and H Grant, 'Why diverse teams are smarter', *Harvard Business Review*, 2016,

https://hbr.org/2016/11/why-diverse-teams-are-smarter

12. P Kivel, 'Act like a man box', 2007, http://paulkivel.com/wp-content/uploads/2011/09/actlikeamanbox.pdf

13. 'Women in STEM statistics', 2021, www.stemwomen.co.uk/blog/2021/01/women-in-stem-percentages-of-women-in-stem-statistics

14. M Bayern, 'Why more than half of women leave the tech industry', Techrepublic.com, 2019, www.techrepublic.com/article/why-more-than-half-of-women-leave-the-tech-industry

Chapter 1 – What's The Problem?

1. E Burt, 'HR's gender challenge', *People Management*, 2017, www.peoplemanagement.co.uk/long-reads/articles/hr-gender-challenge#_ga=2.52620512.937954061.1585150759-1476279883.1585150759

2. WISE, 'Annual core-STEM stats round up: 2019–20', WISE, 2020, www.wisecampaign.org.uk/statistics/annual-core-stem-stats-round-up-2019-20

3. P Sindwani, 'India tops the world in producing female graduates in STEM but ranks 19th in employing them', *Business Insider India*, 2020, www.businessinsider.in/careers/news/india-tops-the-world-in-producing-female-graduates-in-stem-but-ranks-19th-in-employing-them/articleshow/74117413.cms

4. Catalyst, 'Quick take: Women in science, technology, engineering, and mathematics (STEM)', Catalyst, 2020, www.catalyst.org/research/women-in-science-technology-engineering-and-mathematics-stem/
5. Ibid.
6. E Hinchliffe, 'The number of female CEOs in the Fortune 500 hits an all-time record', *Fortune*, 2020, https://fortune.com/2020/05/18/women-ceos-fortune-500-2020
7. Hampton-Alexander, 'FTSE women leaders', Hampton-Alexander Review, 2019, https://ftsewomenleaders.com/wp-content/uploads/2019/11/HA-Review-Report-2019.pdf
8. H Tsukayama, 'No, really. How do we get girls to code?', *The Washington Post*, 2014, www.washingtonpost.com/news/the-switch/wp/2014/06/19/no-really-how-do-we-get-girls-to-code
9. HM Treasury, 'Empowering productivity: Harnessing the talents of women in financial services', Virgin Money, 2016, https://uk.virginmoney.com/virgin/assets/pdf/Virgin-Money-Empowering-Productivity-Report.pdf
10. The Law Society, 'Women, leadership and the law', The Law Society, 2018, www.lawsociety.org.uk/topics/the-city/women-leadership-and-the-law
11. J Huang et al, 'Women in the workplace 2019', McKinsey and Company, 2019,

www.mckinsey.com / ~ / media / McKinsey / Featured%20Insights / Gender%20Equality / Women%20in%20the%20Workplace%202019 / Women-in-the-workplace-2019.pdf

12. Exhibit from 'Women in the workplace 2020', 2020, McKinsey & Company and LeanIn.Org, www.womenintheworkplace.com. Copyright © 2021 McKinsey & Company and LeanIn.Org. All rights reserved. Reprinted by permission.

13. M Richards and I Waterfield, 'Cracking the Code – a gender intelligent approach to developing corporate leaders', KPMG, 2013, https:// home.kpmg / uk / en / home / insights / 2013 / 12 / cracking-the-code-researchbehavioural-differences-in-the-workplace.html

14. J Weeks, '1921: The year when football banned women', HistoryExtra, 2017, www.historyextra. com / period / first-world-war / 1921-when-football-association-banned-women-soccer-dick-kerr-ladies-lily-parr

15. J Armstrong and J Ghaboos, 'Women collaborating with men: Everyday workplace inclusion', Murray Edwards College, 2019, www.murrayedwards.cam.ac.uk / sites / default / files / files / Everyday%20Workplace%20 Inclusion_FINAL.pdf

16. ME Heilman, 'Gender stereotypes and workplace bias', *Research in Organizational*

Behaviour, 32/1, 2012, 113–135, https://doi.org/10.1016/j.riob.2012.11.003

17. 5c descriptors. Copyright © Jill Armstrong and Zoe Young

18. J Armstrong and J Ghaboos, 'Women collaborating with men: Everyday workplace inclusion', Murray Edwards College, 2019, www.murrayedwards.cam.ac.uk/sites/default/files/files/Everyday%20Workplace%20Inclusion_FINAL.pdf

19. J Armstrong and J Ghaboos, 'Women collaborating with men: Everyday workplace inclusion', Murray Edwards College, 2019, www.murrayedwards.cam.ac.uk/sites/default/files/files/Everyday%20Workplace%20Inclusion_FINAL.pdf. Design by Georgia King Design.

20. Ibid.

21. Ibid.

22. KP Jones, 'Isms and schisms: A meta-analysis of the prejudice-discrimination relationship across racism, sexism, and ageism', *Journal of Organizational Behaviour*, 38/7, 2017, 1076–1100, https://doi.org/10.1002/job.2187

23. 'The true scale of the crisis facing working mums', Pregnant Then Screwed, 2020, https://pregnantthenscrewed.com/childcare-covid-and-career

24. S Sanders, 'Childbearing for women born in different years, England and Wales: 2018', Office for National Statistics, 2019,

www.ons.gov.uk/peoplepopulationand
community/birthsdeathsandmarriages/
conceptionandfertilityrates/bulletins/
childbearingforwomenbornindifferent
yearsenglandandwales/2018

25. R Umoh, 'A recent study says some white men
    feel excluded at work', CNBC, 2017, www.cnbc.
    com/2017/10/12/a-recent-study-says-some-
    white-men-feel-excluded-at-work.html

26. SJ Dubner, 'Episode 280: Why is my life
    so hard?', Freakonomics, 2017, https://
    freakonomics.com/podcast/why-is-my-life-so-
    hard

27. S Davidai and T Gilovich, 'The headwinds/
    tailwinds asymmetry: An availability bias in
    assessments of barriers and blessings', *Journal
    of Personality and Social Psychology*, 111/6, 2016,
    835–851, https://doi.org/10.1037/pspa0000066

28. J Prime and CA Moss-Racusin, 'Report: Engaging
    men in gender initiatives: What change agents
    need to know', Catalyst, 2009, www.catalyst.org/
    research/engaging-men-in-gender-initiatives-
    what-change-agents-need-to-know

29. R Sutherland, 'Tackling the root causes of
    suicide', NHS England, 2018, www.england.nhs.
    uk/blog/tackling-the-root-causes-of-suicide

30. American Foundation for Suicide Protection,
    'Suicide statistics', American Foundation for
    Suicide Protection, 2020, https://afsp.org/
    suicide-statistics

31. J Snowden, 'Indian suicide data: What do they mean?', *Indian Journal of Medical Research*, 150/4, 2019, 315–320, https://doi.org/10.4103/ijmr. IJMR_1367_19

Chapter 2 – Engaging Men As Allies

1. National Centre for Women In Technology, 'Sitting to take a stand', University of Colorado, 2019, www.sitwithme.org

2. TV2, 'All that we share', 2017, www.youtube. com/watch?v=jD8tjhVO1Tc

3. 'Privilege/class/social inequalities explained in a $100 race', 2018, www.youtube.com/ watch?v=4K5fbQ1-zps

4. D Spira, 'Exploring privilege by throwing bits of paper: An improved exercise', 2015, https:// danspira.com/2015/01/06/exploring-privilege-by-throwing-bits-of-paper-an-improved-exercise

5. J Prime and CA Moss-Racusin, 'Report: Engaging men in gender initiatives: What change agents need to know', Catalyst, 2009, www.catalyst.org/ research/engaging-men-in-gender-initiatives-what-change-agents-need-to-know

6. V Hunt, D Layton and S Prince, 'Why diversity matters', McKinsey and Company, 2015, www.mckinsey.com/business-functions/ organization/our-insights/why-diversity-matters

7. C Ashcroft and A Breitzmann, 'Who invents IT? An analysis of women's participation in information technology patenting', National Centre for Women in Information Technology, 2006, www.ncwit.org/sites/default/files/resources/patentreport_wappendix.pdf

8. Corporate Leadership Council, 'Creating competitive advantage through workforce diversity', Corporate Leadership Council, 2012, https://s3.amazonaws.com/texassports_com/documents/2014/11/24/corporate_leadership_council_report.pdf

9. A Farnham, 'Female crash dummies injured more: What car should women buy?', ABC News, 2012, https://abcnews.go.com/Business/female-crash-dummies-injured/story?id=16004267

10. C Criado-Perez, 'The deadly truth about a world built for men – from stab vests to car crashes', *The Guardian*, 2019, www.theguardian.com/lifeandstyle/2019/feb/23/truth-world-built-for-men-car-crashes

11. C Porterfield, 'A lot of PPE doesn't fit women – and in the coronavirus pandemic, it puts them in danger', *Forbes*, 2020, www.forbes.com/sites/carlieporterfield/2020/04/29/a-lot-of-ppe-doesnt-fit-women-and-in-the-coronavirus-pandemic-it-puts-them-in-danger/?sh=9851371315a0

12. T Poletti, 'Opinion: Apple Watch isn't what women want', MarketWatch, 2014, www.marketwatch.com/story/apple-watch-isnt-what-women-want-2014-09-11

13. BBC, 'Apple's "sexist" credit card investigated by US regulator', BBC, 2019, www.bbc.co.uk/news/business-50365609

14. E Tutchell and J Edmonds, *Man-Made: Why so few women are in positions of power*, Routledge, 2015

15. CH Tinsley and RJ Ely, 'What most people get wrong about men and women', *Harvard Business Review*, 2018, https://hbr.org/2018/05/what-most-people-get-wrong-about-men-and-women

16. J Terrell et al, 'Gender differences and bias in open source: Pull request acceptance of women versus men', *PeerJ Computer Science*, 3/111, 2017, https://doi.org/10.7717/peerj-cs.111

17. F Dobbin and A Kalev, 'Why doesn't diversity training work?', *Harvard Ed.*, 2018, https://scholar.harvard.edu/files/dobbin/files/an2018.pdf

Chapter 3 – Challenging Male Mindsets

1. J Armstrong and J Ghaboos, 'Women collaborating with men: Everyday workplace inclusion', Murray Edwards College, 2019,

www.murrayedwards.cam.ac.uk/sites/
default/files/files/Everyday%20Workplace%20
Inclusion_FINAL.pdf

2. SK Johnson and DR Hekman, 'Women and
minorities are penalized for promoting
diversity', *Harvard Business Review*, 2016,
https://hbr.org/2016/03/women-and-
minorities-are-penalized-for-promoting-
diversity

3. F Dobbin and A Kalev, 'Why diversity programs
fail', *Harvard Business Review*, 2016, https://hbr.
org/2016/07/why-diversity-programs-fail

4. TS Mohr, 'Why women don't apply for jobs
unless they're 100% qualified', *Harvard Business
Review*, 2014, https://hbr.org/2014/08/why-
women-dont-apply-for-jobs-unless-theyre-100-
qualified

5. M Kimmel, 'Why gender equality is good for
everyone – men included', TED Talks, 2015,
www.ted.com/talks/michael_kimmel_why_
gender_equality_is_good_for_everyone_men_
included?language=en

6. Fightingsailor, 'The case for inclusive
leadership', 2020, https://fightingsailor.
wordpress.com/2020/07/28/the-case-for-
inclusive-leadership-or-to-give-it-its-proper-
title-leadership

Chapter 4 – Tackling Bias To Build Inclusive Teams

1. L Babcock, MP Recalde and L Vesterlund, 'Why women volunteer for tasks that don't lead to promotions', *Harvard Business Review*, 2018, https://hbr.org/2018/07/why-women-volunteer-for-tasks-that-dont-lead-to-promotions

2. A Player et al, 'Overlooked leadership potential: The preference for leadership potential in job candidates who are men vs. women', *Frontiers in Psychology*, 2019. https://doi.org/10.3389/fpsyg.2019.00755

3. ME Heilman, 'Gender stereotypes and workplace bias', *Research in Organizational Behaviour*, 32/1, 2012, 113–135, https://doi.org/10.1016/j.riob.2012.11.003

4. BBC, 'US Open: What was Serena Williams' row with the umpire all about?', BBC, 2018, www.bbc.co.uk/newsround/45469693

5. CF Karpowitz and T Mendelberg, *The Silent Sex*, Princeton University Press, 2014

6. C Leaper and L Ayres, 'A meta-analytic review of gender variations in adults' language use: Talkativeness, affiliative speech, and assertive speech', *Personality and Social Psychology Review*, 11/4, 2007, 328–363, https://doi.org/10.1177/1088868307302221

7. AB Hancock and BA Rubin, 'Influence of communication partner's gender on

language', *Journal of Language and Social Psychology*, 34/1, 2014, 46–64, https://doi.org/10.1177/0261927X14533197

8. D Glover, A Pallais and W Pariente, 'Discrimination as a self-fulfilling prophecy: Evidence from French grocery stores', *Quarterly Journal of Economics*, 2017, 132/3, 1219–1260, https://doi.org/10.1093/qje/qjx006

9. O Petter, *'What is Hepeating?'*, *The Independent*, 2017, www.independent.co.uk/life-style/hepeating-what-woman-ignore-men-idea-repeat-sexism-misogynist-a8080601.html

10. Advisory Board, 'How often are women interrupted by men? Here's what the research says', Advisory Board, 2017, www.advisory.com/daily-briefing/2017/07/07/men-interrupting-women

11. C Collins, 'Helping women ensure their voices are heard', BBC, 2017, www.bbc.co.uk/news/business-42253091

12. PM Fabiano et al, 'Engaging men as social justice allies in ending violence against women: Evidence for a social norms approach', *Journal of American College Health*, 52/3, 2003, 105–112, https://doi.org/10.1080/07448480309595732

13. J Armstrong and J Ghaboos, 'Women collaborating with men: Everyday workplace inclusion', Murray Edwards College, 2019, www.murrayedwards.cam.ac.uk/sites/default/files/files/Everyday%20Workplace%20Inclusion_FINAL.pdf

Chapter 5 – Improving The Hiring Process

1. Office for National Statistics, 'Gender pay gap in the UK: 2020', ONS, 2020, www.ons.gov.uk/employmentandlabourmarket/peopleinwork/earningsandworkinghours/bulletins/genderpaygapintheuk/2020

2. A Krivkovich et al, 'Women in the workplace 2020', McKinsey and Company, 2020, www.mckinsey.com/featured-insights/diversity-and-inclusion/women-in-the-workplace

3. A Singal, 'Why women at C-Suite level are double the loyal to an organization than men', Entrepreneur India, 2018, www.entrepreneur.com/article/320935

4. D Sundheim, 'Do women take as many risks as men?', *Harvard Business Review*, 2013, https://hbr.org/2013/02/do-women-take-as-many-risks-as

5. B Pawlowski, R Atwal and RIM Dunbar, 'Sex differences in everyday risk-taking behaviour in humans', *Evolutionary Psychology*, 6/1, 2008, 29–42, https://doi.org/10.1177/147470490800600104

6. S Sandberg, *Lean In*, Random House, 2013

7. TS Mohr, 'Why women don't apply for jobs unless they're 100% qualified', *Harvard Business Review*, 2014, https://hbr.org/2014/08/why-women-dont-apply-for-jobs-unless-theyre-100-qualified

8. M Ignatova, 'New report: Women apply to fewer jobs than men but are more likely to get hired', LinkedIn, 2019, https://business.linkedin.com/talent-solutions/blog/diversity/2019/how-women-find-jobs-gender-report

9. R Ely and I Padavic, 'What's really holding women back?', *Harvard Business Review*, Mar–Apr 2020, https://hbr.org/2020/03/whats-really-holding-women-back

10. Glassdoor, '10 ways to remove gender bias from job descriptions', Glassdoor, 2017, www.glassdoor.com/employers/blog/10-ways-remove-gender-bias-job-listings

11. BBC News, 'Amazon scrapped "sexist AI" tool', BBC, 2018, www.bbc.co.uk/news/technology-45809919

12. A Webber, 'Study finds "alarming" bias against minority ethnic candidates', *Personnel Today*, 2019, www.personneltoday.com/hr/study-finds-alarming-discrimination-against-minority-ethnic-candidates

13. D Meyer, 'Amazon reportedly killed an AI recruitment system because it couldn't stop the tool from discriminating against women', *Fortune*, 2018, https://fortune.com/2018/10/10/amazon-ai-recruitment-bias-women-sexist

14. BBC News, 'Amazon scrapped "sexist AI" tool', BBC, 2018, www.bbc.co.uk/news/technology-45809919

15. J Dastin, 'Amazon scraps secret AI recruiting tool that showed bias against women', Reuters.com, 2018, www.reuters.com/article/us-amazon-com-jobs-automation-insight-idUSKCN1MK08G

16. C Goldin and C Rouse, 'Orchestrating impartiality: The impact of "blind" auditions on female musicians', National Bureau of Economic Research, 1997, www.nber.org/papers/w5903

17. M Blair-Loy et al, 'Gender in engineering departments: Are there gender differences in interruptions of academic job talks?', *Social Sciences*, 6/1, 2017, 29, https://doi.org/10.3390/socsci6010029

18. T Jacobs, 'Men are judged based on their potential; women are judged based on their past performance', *Pacific Standard*, 2019, https://psmag.com/economics/men-are-judged-based-on-their-potential-women-are-judged-based-on-their-past-performance

19. I Bohnet, *What Works: Gender equality by design*, Harvard University Press, 2016

20. Ibid.

21. Glassdoor, 'Salary and benefits are most important for US workers and job seekers looking at job ads, according to Glassdoor survey', Glassdoor, 2018, www.glassdoor.com/about-us/salary-and-benefits-are-most-important-for-u-s-workers-and-job-seekers-looking-at-job-ads-according-to-glassdoor-survey

Chapter 6 – Retaining Talent And Managing Careers

1. SJ Correll and C Simmard, 'Research: Vague feedback is holding women back', *Harvard Business Review*, 2016, https://hbr.org/2016/04/research-vague-feedback-is-holding-women-back

2. J Guo, 'Why men get all the credit when they work with women', *Washington Post*, 2015, www.washingtonpost.com/news/wonk/wp/2015/11/13/why-men-get-all-the-credit-when-they-work-with-women

3. R Ely and I Padavic, 'What's really holding women back?', *Harvard Business Review*, Mar–Apr 2020, https://hbr.org/2020/03/whats-really-holding-women-back

4. H Ibarra, NM Carter and C Silva, 'Why men still get more promotions than women', *Harvard Business Review*, 2010, https://hbr.org/2010/09/why-men-still-get-more-promotions-than-women

5. S Nadkani and EYN Oon, 'The rise of women in society: Enablers and inhibitors – a global study', Cambridge Judge Business School, 2015, https://issuu.com/cambridgejbs/docs/bnywomenomics-cambridge-research

6. J Armstrong, 'Inclusive networking and sponsorship', Murray Edwards College, 2019, www.murrayedwards.cam.ac.uk/sites/default/files/files/Inclusive%20Networking%20and%20Sponsorship_FINAL.pdf

7. SG Carmichael, 'The research is clear: Long hours backfire for people and for companies', *Harvard Business Review*, 2015, https://hbr.org/2015/08/the-research-is-clear-long-hours-backfire-for-people-and-for-companies

8. J Kodz, B Kersley and MT Strebler, 'Breaking the long hours culture', The Institute for Employment Studies, 1998, www.employment-studies.co.uk/system/files/resources/files/352.pdf

9. CC Miller, 'The 24/7 work culture's toll on families and gender equality', *New York Times*, 2015, www.nytimes.com/2015/05/31/upshot/the-24-7-work-cultures-toll-on-families-and-gender-equality.html

10. R Ely and I Padavic, 'What's really holding women back?', *Harvard Business Review*, Mar–Apr 2020, https://hbr.org/2020/03/whats-really-holding-women-back

11. G Pitcher, 'Seeking gender balance: How contractors are reinventing themselves', *Construction News*, 2019, www.constructionnews.co.uk/agenda/seeking-gender-balance-contractors-reinventing-26-11-2019

12. M Bryant, 'More fathers are taking paternity leave, but mothers are still doing all the work', *The Guardian*, 2019, www.theguardian.com/money/2019/nov/17/more-fathers-are-taking-paternity-leave-but-mothers-are-still-doing-all-the-work

13. S Zalis, 'Men should take parental leave –
    here's why', *Forbes*, 2018, www.forbes.
    com/sites/shelleyzalis/2018/05/03/
    why-mandatory-parental-leave-is-good-for-
    business/?sh=21e01f2f9ded
14. BBC, 'Paternity leave: "All of my dad friends
    were incredibly jealous"', BBC, 2019, www.bbc.
    co.uk/news/business-47792269
15. Aviva, 'Parental leave', Aviva, 2020, www.aviva.
    co.uk/aviva-edit/surveys-and-reports/articles/
    parental-leave-survey

Chapter 7 – Promotion And Compensation Processes

1. G Charness and U Gneezy, 'Strong evidence
   for gender differences in risk taking', *Journal of
   Economic Behaviour & Organization*, 83/1
   2012, 50–58, https://doi.org/10.1016/
   j.jebo.2011.06.007
2. McKinsey and Company and LeanIn.org,
   'Women in the workplace 2019', McKinsey
   and Company, 2020, https://wiw-report.
   s3.amazonaws.com/Women_in_the_
   Workplace_2019.pdf
3. C Dwyer, '12 common biases that affect how
   we make everyday decisions', *Psychology Today*,
   2018, www.psychologytoday.com/us/blog/
   thoughts-thinking/201809/12-common-biases-
   affect-how-we-make-everyday-decisions

4. 'Why men get all the credit when they work with women', *Washington Post*, 2015, www.washingtonpost.com/news/wonk/wp/2015/11/13/why-men-get-all-the-credit-when-they-work-with-women
5. https://sitwithme.org
6. Office of National Statistics, 'Gender pay gap in the UK: 2019', ONS, 2019, www.ons.gov.uk/employmentandlabourmarket/peopleinwork/earningsandworkinghours/bulletins/genderpaygapintheuk/2019
7. Barclays, 'Pay gaps report 2019', Barclays, 2019, https://home.barclays/content/dam/home-barclays/documents/investor-relations/reports-and-events/annual-reports/2019/Barclays%20Pay%20Gaps%20Report%202019.pdf
8. K McCarthy, 'Satya "Karma" Nadella ignored our complaints over pay gap, thousands of Microsoft women say', *The Register*, 2019, www.theregister.com/2019/11/06/microsoft_pay_gap_ninth_circuit

Chapter 8 – The Way Forward: A Manifesto For Change

1. Corporate Leadership Council, 'Creating competitive advantage through workforce diversity', Corporate Leadership Council, 2012, https://s3.amazonaws.com/texassports_com/documents/2014/11/24/corporate_leadership_council_report.pdf

2. SR Levine, 'Diversity confirmed to boost innovation and financial results', *Forbes*, 2020, www.forbes.com / sites / forbesinsights / 2020 / 01 / 15 / diversity-confirmed-to-boost-innovation-and-financial-results

3. J Hempel, 'Satya Nadella on growth mindsets: "The learn-it-all does better than the know-it-all"', 2019, www.linkedin.com / pulse / satya-nadella-growth-mindsets-learn-it-all-does-better-jessi-hempel

Acknowledgements

The authors thank their families for their unstinting support before and during the writing of this book. You are our guiding lights for all the work that we do and this book would never have been possible without you.

We also thank all of the colleagues and friends we have worked with over the years who have continually encouraged us to try and make a difference with the work we do. As we say in this book, it is a marathon not a sprint and your support is what kept us running. Your patience and insight have also helped us when we made mistakes, and made sure we keep practising being better allies to everyone in the workplace.

Finally, thanks to Lucy, Roger, Kate, Abi and everyone at the Rethink team for their help in getting this book to see the light of day. You did an amazing job bringing coherence to our different voices.

The Authors

 **Gary Ford** has more than thirty years' experience in the IT industry in financial services. Most recently, Gary was a managing director at a large US financial services organisation, where he managed a number of enterprise-wide software delivery programmes.

In Q1 2020, Gary started his own consultancy business which, as well as providing IT and wider business solutions, delivers inclusion training and helps organisations create allies networks. He is currently working as CEO and COO of two new business ventures in the education sector.

Stephen Koch has twenty-seven years' experience in investment banking IT at a number of major financial services firms. He has spent most of his career building risk management systems and managing global technology development teams. Up until recently, he was a managing director at the same large US financial services firm as Gary. He is now Director of Demographics at NHS-Digital.

In 2016, Gary and Stephen co-founded the firm's Male Allies programme for Women in Technology. Together they grew this network from a small group of people to a firm-wide network of allies across the whole organisation. This included developing an inclusion workshop that has been run over 200 times across six countries and has trained more than 2,000 allies. The programme has now been adopted across all business areas and the investment banking division recently started rolling out an updated version of the workshop.

Both Stephen and Gary were shortlisted for the 2019 Everywoman Male Agent of Change award.

 **Dr Jill Armstrong** was a Bye-Fellow at Murray Edwards College, University of Cambridge from 2016 to 2020, where she led the 'Collaborating with Men' action research programme. Jill has published a number of reports, including 'Everyday workplace inclusion', on engaging men and suggesting practical actions to take.

Jill writes, speaks, lectures and consults on gender inclusion and works with organisations on everyday inclusion tactics. Jill has also written *Like Mother, Like Daughter?: How career women influence their daughters' ambition*, which was published in 2017 by Policy Press.

Previously, she was a founding director of two successful commercial market research companies.

www.theaccidentalsexist.com